The Villainization of America

How a Nation Was Taught to Hate Itself

Richard Lowe
The Writing King

Enemies of You Series
https://enemiesofyou.com

The Villainization of America: How a Nation Was Taught to Hate Itself

Copyright © 2026 by Richard G Lowe

Disclaimer

This book presents the author's analysis and opinions based on publicly available information, documented historical events, and published research. While every effort has been made to ensure accuracy, some details may have changed since publication. The examples and arguments cited represent the author's conclusions from available evidence. Readers are encouraged to consult primary sources and conduct their own research. Views expressed are solely those of the author and do not constitute legal, political, or professional advice.

Table of Contents

See books by Richard Lowe at

https://masterofworlds.com

Get free publishing insights and industry updates at

https://thewritingking.substack.com

For ghostwriting and book coaching services see

https://thewritingking.com

Enemies of You Series

The Death of Thinking
The Enslavement of Humanity

The Birth of the Augmented Human
The Freeing of Humanity

Turn Off The TV, Get Off Your Ass, and Do Something

Stuck in the Middle
Wars, Weapons, and the Forces That Will Shape the Next Thirty Years

The Enshittification of America
How Private Equity Destroyed the Things We Love

The Emasculation of America
How Russia's Long War Against the American Male Is Destroying the Nation From Within

Everybody's Prejudiced
How We Judge, Why We Do It, and What Rational People Choose to Do About It

The Villainization of America

———

See the full series description at the back of this book.

A Note to the Reader

Something is being done to this country. I want to be clear about that before anything else. Not something that happened. Something that is happening now, deliberately, by identifiable actors, with identifiable goals. This book is my account of what it is, who is doing it, and what it is going to cost us if we do not name it clearly enough to fight it.

America has a real history. Parts of that history are genuinely shameful. I am not here to pretend otherwise. Slavery happened. The dispossession of indigenous peoples happened. Jim Crow happened. The failures are real and they belong in any honest account of what this country is. I am not disputing any of that.

What I am disputing is the operation that uses those real failures to build something different: a permanent indictment. Not a reckoning, which names what went wrong and points toward repair. An indictment, which names what went wrong and declares the whole project irredeemable. That operation is not honest history. It is a weapon. And it is being used against the country my grandfather nearly died for.

Some of the people running this operation believe what they are saying. Others know exactly what they are doing. The foreign governments funding and amplifying it know exactly what they are doing. I am not interested in sorting out who is naive and who is cynical. I am interested in documenting what the operation is, how it works, and what it has already produced.

If you love this country and want to understand what is being done to it, this is your book. If you have concluded that America is simply evil, this book will not help you. The evidence does not support that conclusion, and I am not going to pretend it does.

Preface

My grandfather spent three and a half years in a Japanese prisoner of war camp. He was Navy. He survived things that I will not describe here because he described them himself, in his own words, in a memoir I helped him publish called Behind the Wire. When I ask myself why I wrote this book, that memoir is part of the answer.

He would talk about what happened to him. That was not the problem. The problem was that nobody wanted to listen. Not because they didn't care about him. They cared. The problem was that the story made them uncomfortable, and after a while people get tired of being uncomfortable, and so the man who had survived three and a half years in a camp sat with his stories mostly in silence, and I was the one who listened, and eventually I was the one who helped him get the words onto a page where they could not be ignored.

What he survived, he survived for a specific reason. Not an abstract one. A concrete one. He believed the country he was fighting for was worth fighting for. That belief was not naive. He knew what America was. He had grown up in it and understood its failures and its contradictions. He was not blind. He knew the country he was fighting for was not perfect. He believed it was the best thing going on this earth, and that what it represented was worth his life if it came to that. None of that changed his conclusion about whether it was worth three and a half years in a camp. He came home, he lived his life, and he died believing the same thing he believed when he shipped out.

I grew up in California. I no longer live there. Those two sentences tell you something about the last thirty years. The California I grew up in and the California that exists now are not the same place in any way that matters beyond the geography. What happened to it is not a mystery. It is, in fact, the subject of this book. The most populated state in the country became, over the course of my lifetime, one of the clearest examples of what happens when the institutions responsible for transmitting a national story stop believing the story is worth transmitting.

I have watched this process from different angles across several decades. I watched it as a young man in California when it was mostly confined to universities and certain neighborhoods in certain cities. I watched it accelerate in the 1990s when the academic framework started showing up in newspapers and television. I watched the brief interruption of September 11, 2001, when the country remembered for a moment what it was and what it was capable of, and then I watched the memory of that day fade and the process resume with more momentum than before. In the last ten years, with social media providing both a distribution system and a measurement tool, the process has become impossible to look away from.

Every day the news is full of stories about America being a bad country. Stories about its founding, its history, its military, its symbols, its institutions. Some of those stories contain real facts about real failures. Some of them are doing something else entirely. This book is about how to tell the difference, who built the machinery that makes the difference hard to see, and what it costs when a country loses the capacity to tell its own story honestly.

My grandfather's story is honest. It includes things that are hard to read. It does not conclude that the country he served was not worth serving. He came home and built a life here and he believed, until the end, that this place was worth what he paid for it.

I am angry about what is being done to that story. Not sad. Angry. There is a difference. Sad is what you feel when something is over. Anger is what you feel when something is still happening and you can still do something about it.

This book is what I can do about it.

Richard Lowe
Florida, 2026

Introduction: The Story That Replaces the Country

I grew up in California and I live in Florida now. The distance between those two places, as an American experience, is larger than the geography suggests. In California, in the cities I knew, the default attitude toward American identity has shifted in my lifetime from something taken for granted to something contested to something many people treat as a source of embarrassment. In Florida, at least in the communities I move through, the flag on the front porch still means what it used to mean. The veteran who served is still someone the neighborhood knows and respects. The story of what America is and what it has been worth, while not uncritical, is still a story people are willing to tell.

I notice the difference every day. It is not a political observation. It is a civic one. The California I left had communities where the basic architecture of American shared identity had been so thoroughly dismantled, in the schools, in the media, in the professional culture, that the people living there could not agree on what they were part of. The Florida I live in has not been immune to the process this book documents, but it has resisted more of it, and the resistance is visible in how people talk about themselves and their country.

That difference between places is what this book is about at the ground level. The argument is national and in some ways international. But the thing the argument produces, at the level where it touches people's lives, is the difference between a community that believes it is part of something worth belonging to and a community that has been taught it is not.

Every nation runs on a story. Not a myth in the sense of something false, but a narrative that tells its people who they are, where they came from, what they stand for, and why any of it matters. The story does not have to be flattering. It does not have to omit the failures. What it has to do is hold together. It has to give people a reason to participate in the collective project, to pay taxes and obey laws and raise children who will do the same, and, when necessary, to put on a uniform and go somewhere dangerous on behalf of people they have never met.

Remove that story and you do not get citizens. You get residents. People who are physically present in a geography but who have no particular stake in whether the institutions that organize that geography survive. That distinction matters in peacetime. It is decisive in a crisis.

The United States has been running, for several decades now, a large and well-funded operation to replace its story. The operation was not planned by a single actor, does not have a central director, and does not require coordination between its many participants. What it has instead is convergence. Academic frameworks developed by people with genuine intellectual ambitions. Political movements with genuine grievances. Media institutions that adopted those frameworks and those grievances and made them the default lens through which American public life is interpreted. Foreign adversaries who recognized in all of this a weapon that American institutions were building for them, and who applied their own resources to making it sharper.

Let me tell you the new story. The one being taught in the schools and assumed in the newsroom and enforced in the corporate training program. America was founded in sin, slavery and stolen land, and that sin is structural, baked into every institution, every outcome. The founding ideals were a cover story for power, not a genuine aspiration. The military is a machine of empire. Religion is a tool of control. Capitalism is exploitation with a flag on it. Individual achievement is a myth or a function of privilege. The flag means the dead, not the dream. The anthem is a provocation.

This is the story being taught to American children. Right now. In schools their parents pay taxes to fund.

This book is about that replacement. Not about whether America deserves criticism, because it does. Every country does. This book is about the specific operation by which criticism of genuine failures became a totalized narrative of irredeemable evil. Who built that narrative. Who funds it. Who amplifies it. What it produces when it reaches the people who are supposed to believe that what they are part of is worth something.

Reckoning and Villainization Are Not the Same Thing

The most important distinction in this book is between reckoning and villainization. They look similar from the outside. Both involve naming failures. Both make people uncomfortable. Both encounter resistance from people who would rather not examine difficult history. But they are aimed at different targets and produce different outcomes.

Reckoning says: this is what happened, this is why it happened, this is the damage it did, and this is what repair looks like. Reckoning is the process by which Germany confronted what it did between 1933 and 1945. It is painful and necessary and it produces something on the other side: a society that has genuinely processed its worst chapter and built something better on the other side of it.

Villainization says: this is what happened, and it proves what this country is at its core, and no amount of change can alter that fundamental nature, and anyone who defends any aspect of what was built here is either naive or complicit. Villainization does not aim at repair. It aims at indictment. And indictment is not a process with an end. It is a permanent condition that forecloses the possibility of the thing being indicted ever being worth defending.

The distinction matters because the two operations produce entirely different citizens. Reckoning produces people who understand their country's failures, work to address them, and maintain the belief that the project is worth continuing. Villainization produces people who have been taught that the project is not worth continuing. And a country full of people who do not believe the project is worth continuing is a country that cannot defend itself.

Every chapter will return to that distinction, because the conflation of the two is the primary defense mechanism of the villainization operation. Call it villainization and the response is always: how dare you, we are just telling the truth about history. That response works as long as nobody draws the line between honest truth-telling and strategic indictment. This book draws the line.

The Convergence

No single actor built the villainization of America. That is the first thing to understand and the most important. This is not a story about a conspiracy. It is a story about convergence, about independent forces that developed for entirely different reasons, arrived at similar conclusions about what America's story should be, and amplified each other's effects without coordination.

The academic frameworks came first, developed by genuine scholars with genuine intellectual programs, most of them working in good faith on real problems of race, gender, and power. The critical theory that arrived from Europe, the Black radical tradition that engaged with American history from the perspective of those who had been excluded from its promises, the feminist theory that named real structures of inequality. None of these traditions were invented by foreign actors. None of them required Soviet direction. All of them produced insights worth taking seriously.

What happened to them in the American university system is what this book documents. They were extended, systematized, institutionalized, and eventually deployed in ways that went far beyond their original intellectual purposes. The specific threads that were most useful for producing a totalized indictment of America were pulled out and amplified. The threads that pointed toward repair and continuation were allowed to atrophy. The result, by the 1990s and 2000s, was an academic apparatus that produced not scholars who understood American failures and worked toward American improvement, but scholars who had concluded that the American project itself was the problem.

The media absorbed those scholars. The corporations hired those graduates. The political movements found in those frameworks a vocabulary for mobilization that proved extraordinarily effective. And throughout all of it, beginning in the 1960s with Soviet active measures and continuing through the Internet Research Agency's social media operations documented in the Senate Intelligence Committee reports, foreign adversaries identified the villainization narrative as a weapon worth funding and amplifying.

They did not build it. They did not need to. They needed only to recognize what it was doing and put their thumb on the scale.

They just had to find it and push.

What This Book Is

A veteran who cannot explain to his son why he served. An immigrant whose grandchildren have been taught to pity her for choosing America. A nun who runs a food pantry while the foundations that could fund her require data reports her clients cannot read. These people are in this book. So is the data that describes what produced them.

What this book is not is an argument that America should be immune from criticism. Every country should be criticized when it fails to live up to its own stated ideals. America fails at that regularly and the failures should be named and addressed. What this book argues is that naming failures for the purpose of producing repair is a different operation from naming failures to produce indictment. The first is patriotism at its best. The second is, at minimum, useful to America's enemies, and, at maximum, something considerably worse.

Before proceeding, this book owes its strongest critics an honest hearing. The most serious version of the opposing argument is not that the villainization of America is good. It is that the history of how American institutions were built and maintained IS the history of racial exclusion, not a detour from the founding ideals but a feature of how those ideals were implemented, and that fully documenting that history is itself a form of patriotism. This argument has serious scholars behind it. It is not the same as saying America is evil. It is saying that you cannot honestly transmit the founding ideals without transmitting the full story of how those ideals were withheld from specific people for specific reasons across specific decades. On this point, the serious version of the opposing argument is correct.

History of exclusion belongs in the account. This book does not dispute that. What this book disputes is the extension of that accurate historical claim into the further claim that the founding ideals themselves were fraudulent, that the institutions built on them are not worth improving, and that anyone who defends any aspect of what was built here is defending the exclusion rather than the ideal. That extension does not follow from the historical evidence. The evidence shows a country that has consistently, if imperfectly, expanded the application of its founding ideals to groups previously excluded from them. That expansion is itself the story. The villainization framework cannot account for it because accounting for it would complicate the indictment.

The story of America is not over. It is being contested, right now, in the curriculum and the newsroom and the training room and the social media feed. This book is one account of what that contest looks like and who is winning it.

The people who want America to believe it is evil are counting on Americans not noticing what they are doing until it is too late to matter. This book is for the people who have noticed.

Part One: The Targets

What the operation decided to call evil, and why those specific targets.

Chapter 1: The Founding

I have been reading about the rewriting of American history on social media for years now. Not looking for it. It finds me. The cumulative weight of it is what finally got my attention, not any single story or post. Any single one I could dismiss. The aggregate is harder to dismiss. Story after story, week after week, the same basic message delivered in a hundred different forms: the founding was a fraud, the founders were criminals, the ideals were cover stories, the institutions they built were instruments of oppression dressed up in the language of liberty.

There is honest history and there is this. The people doing the rewriting will tell you they are the same thing. They are not. This chapter shows the difference, and I want to name that plainly before the documentation begins, because the conflation is deliberate. Calling it honest history is how it gets into the classrooms.

The other thing I noticed, and this one cuts deeper than the rest, is what happened to September 11.

I watched it live. I was watching television when the second plane hit and I understood immediately what it was and I sat there and I cried. Not performance. Not shock. Grief. The grief you feel when something you love is attacked. That is what I felt. I was not alone in feeling it. The country felt it together, for a few weeks, in a way I had never seen before and have not seen since. The flags everywhere. Strangers talking to each other. A shared understanding that something had been done to us, to all of us, as Americans, and that we were going to face it together.

That feeling did not last. Within a few years it was gone, replaced first by argument about the response to the attacks and then, as the decade passed, by something I find genuinely hard to describe without getting angry. A revisionist account of what the attacks meant. Who was really responsible. What America had done to deserve them.

Deserve them.

Young people today are being taught a version of September 11 in which the attacks were a response to American foreign policy, American arrogance, American imperial violence. The people who jumped from the towers are background. The framework is foreground. The unity of those first days, which was one of the most human things I have ever witnessed, has been processed into embarrassment by the people who are responsible for transmitting this country's story to the next generation. I watched that shift happen in the media I consumed and I have not forgotten it, and I am not willing to pretend it did not happen.

In 1619, a ship arrived off the coast of Virginia carrying enslaved Africans. That fact is historical. It is documented. It belongs in any honest account of American history. The people on that ship were human beings treated as property, and what was done to them and to the generations that followed them was one of the great crimes in the history of the Western world.

The 1619 Project was responding to something real, and that deserves acknowledgment before the argument begins. For most of the twentieth century, the standard American history curriculum underrepresented the experience and contributions of Black Americans, treated slavery as a regrettable footnote rather than a central institution of the antebellum economy, and glossed over the systematic violence of Jim Crow and its long aftermath. Those were genuine failures of American history education, and the effort to correct them was legitimate. The question this chapter examines is not whether the history of slavery and its legacy belongs at the center of American history education. It does. The question is whether correcting a failure of inclusion requires replacing the entire story with a different one, and whether the replacement story the 1619 Project offered was historically accurate. On both counts, the answer is no.

In 2019, the New York Times Magazine launched a project built on that fact. The 1619 Project proposed to reframe American history entirely around the date of that ship's arrival, arguing that the American founding should be understood not as 1776 but as 1619, that the Revolution was fought primarily to preserve slavery, that the defining features of American democracy are traceable not to the ideals of the Enlightenment but to the institution of slavery and its aftermath. The original landing page stated: the project aims to reframe the country's history, understanding 1619 as our true founding. That phrase, true founding, was quietly removed from the website without announcement or correction after the controversy began.

The project was not a work of scholarship. It was a work of advocacy dressed in the clothes of scholarship. The central factual claim of the lead essay, that protecting slavery was a primary reason colonists fought the American Revolution, was challenged in December 2019 by five of the most distinguished historians in the country: Gordon Wood of Brown, James McPherson of Princeton, Sean Wilentz of Princeton, Victoria Bynum of Texas State, and James Oakes of the City University of New York. All five had spent combined careers of more than 250 years studying precisely the period the essay addressed. Their letter to the Times stated that the essay evinced a displacement of historical understanding by ideology and called the Revolution claim astounding, adding that every statement offered by the project to validate it is false. The Times' editor-in-chief refused to issue corrections.

What followed the refusal is worth documenting precisely. Leslie Harris, a Northwestern historian who had been hired by the Times as a fact-checker for the lead essay, wrote in Politico in March 2020 that she had vigorously warned the Times against the Revolution claim. Despite my advice, the Times published the incorrect statement anyway. That same month the Times issued what it called a clarification, not a correction, changing the language to say that protecting slavery was a primary motivation for some of the colonists. The Pulitzer Center had by this point distributed the 1619 Project curriculum to more than 4,500 classrooms. The curriculum was not recalled when the central claim was walked back.

In 2023, historian James Oakes published a detailed essay in Jacobin, a left-wing publication, documenting that the project had botched the history of the slave economy, misconstrued the origins of Northern economic development, erased the history of antislavery, and rendered emancipation irrelevant. His critique received a fraction of the coverage the original project received.

What the 1619 Project represents is not the arrival of honest history in American education. Honest history was already there. The teaching of slavery and its legacy in American schools had been improving for decades before 2019. By the 1990s, state history standards in most states required substantial treatment of slavery and its legacy. The College Board's 1992 AP United States History framework already centered slavery as a foundational institution. The Library of Congress had been producing primary source collections for classroom use since the 1980s. Textbooks used widely in American high schools by 2010 included chapters on slavery, the failure of Reconstruction, and the civil rights movement that would not have appeared in textbooks twenty years earlier. The improvement was real and documented.

What the 1619 Project represents is the arrival of a specific claim: that the totality of American history is best understood as the working out of the original sin of 1619. That the ideals of the founding were not genuine aspirations but cover stories. That the institutions built on those ideals are therefore not imperfect achievements worth improving but fraudulent constructions worth dismantling.

Howard Zinn and the Long Preparation

The 1619 Project did not arrive in a vacuum. It arrived at the end of a forty-year effort to replace the standard account of American history with what its architects called a people's history, meaning a history told from the perspective of those who had been excluded, exploited, or oppressed by American institutions.

Howard Zinn's A People's History of the United States was the foundational text, published in 1980. Zinn was a historian and activist who had spent his career arguing that conventional American history was a story told by and for the powerful. His book offered an alternative: a history in which Columbus was not an explorer but a slaver, in which the founding fathers were not visionaries but property owners protecting their interests, in which American military history was not a record of defense and sacrifice but of imperial violence.

The book was not a work of balanced scholarship. Zinn said so himself. He acknowledged that he had chosen his evidence to support a thesis and that his thesis was that the American project had been, from its inception, a mechanism of oppression. He was not trying to add complexity to American history. He was trying to replace one story with another.

A People's History sold more than three million copies and became, over the following four decades, one of the most assigned texts in American high schools and colleges. A generation of teachers, journalists, documentary filmmakers, and politicians were educated in a framework in which American history is understood primarily through the lens of who it victimized. That framework, applied consistently over decades, produces a specific kind of citizen: someone who understands American failures with precision and American achievements with skepticism, who can recite the crimes of the founding with accuracy and the ideals of the founding with irony.

Three million copies. Forty years in classrooms. That is not a footnote.

That is not balanced history. Balanced history holds the crimes and the ideals in the same frame and asks what kind of people are capable of both. Zinn's history, and the 1619 Project that followed it, do not ask that question. They answer it in advance: the kind of people who produce this much suffering are not the kind of people whose institutions deserve continuation.

The New Narrative's Own Distortions

The replacement narrative contains an irony that its architects have not grappled with. In correcting one distortion of history, it introduced another one at least as serious. The old American historical narrative erased or minimized the complexity of pre-Columbian Native American life and the full dimensions of what European expansion did to indigenous peoples. Those were genuine failures of honest history. The replacement narrative responded by producing a counter-myth: that pre-contact Native American societies were peaceful, harmonious, and different in kind from the European societies that encountered them. That counter-myth is not history. It is a different kind of propaganda.

The archaeological and anthropological record of pre-Columbian North America documents something far more complex than the counter-myth allows. Lawrence Keeley's War Before Civilization, published in 1996 and based on the archaeological evidence from sites across the world including North America, concluded that tribal warfare was on average twenty times more deadly as a proportion of population than twentieth-century warfare, and that among the indigenous peoples of the Americas, only thirteen percent did not engage in war with their neighbors at least once per year. The Crow Creek site in present-day South Dakota, dated to 1325 AD, contains the remains of 486 people, men, women, and children, an entire town's population, in a mass grave, the bodies showing marks of scalping and mutilation.

Villages throughout the Great Plains were fortified with ditch and palisade defenses, structures requiring enormous communal labor that no community builds without genuine threat of attack. The Iroquois Confederation and the Huron Confederacy, which the replacement narrative often presents as models of indigenous democratic governance, were created precisely to manage the fratricidal inter-tribal wars that had been devastating their societies for generations. Warfare was not something that arrived with Europeans. It was woven into the fabric of pre-Columbian American life.

The evidence for cannibalism in pre-Columbian North America is equally documented and has been equally unwelcome in the environment the replacement narrative created. In 2000, researchers published findings in the journal Nature from the Cowboy Wash site in southwestern Colorado, an ancestral Puebloan location dated to around 1150 AD. The site contained the butchered and cooked remains of seven people, adults, an adolescent, and young children. A coprolite, fossilized human excrement found in a fire pit at the site, tested positive for human myoglobin, a protein found only in skeletal and cardiac muscle cells and not present in the digestive tract. Its presence in the fecal matter meant that someone had consumed human flesh. This was the first direct biochemical evidence of cannibalism at any North American archaeological site, and it was not isolated.

Researchers had already identified more than forty Southwestern sites with human bones showing the same distinctive marks of butchering and cooking. A subsequent excavation in Durango, Colorado uncovered fifteen thousand bone fragments from approximately thirty-five people at a Puebloan site dated to around 800 AD, with the same evidence of cutting, defleshing, and cooking. The Aztec practice of ritual human sacrifice followed by cannibalism is not seriously disputed by mainstream historians of Mesoamerica; the only debate is about its scale.

The Xiximes people of northern Mexico, whose cannibalism the Mexican National Institute of Anthropology and History dismissed as myth as recently as 2008, had that practice confirmed by the institute's own archaeologists in 2011 when excavations produced bones with unmistakable evidence of butchering, defleshing, and cooking. The Karankawa of Texas, the Anasazi of the Southwest, and multiple other groups across the continent left behind physical evidence of practices that the replacement narrative has no framework for.

None of this means that indigenous people were uniquely violent or morally inferior to Europeans. That is precisely the point. They were people. They had warfare because human societies have warfare. Some of them had practices that later generations, including their own descendants, regard as horrific, because human societies throughout history have had practices that later generations regard as horrific. European societies had warfare, torture, human sacrifice in various forms, and practices fully as brutal as anything documented in the pre-Columbian Americas. The comparison is not between noble savages and violent Europeans, or between violent savages and civilized Europeans. The comparison is between two groups of people, both complex, both capable of extraordinary achievement and extraordinary cruelty, who encountered each other under conditions that produced catastrophic outcomes for one of them.

The replacement narrative cannot hold that complexity because its purpose is not to produce honest history but to produce a morality tale. In the morality tale, the people who were harmed must have been innocent, because the severity of the harm requires a proportional innocence to maintain the moral clarity the framework needs. Honest history does not require that innocence. It requires only that we acknowledge what happened to indigenous peoples as one of the great catastrophes of the modern world, driven by disease, deliberate violence, and dispossession, without needing the people involved to have been something other than human.

The villainization of America depends on a villainization of pre-Columbian America's story in reverse. Both distortions serve the same function: they replace the complexity of actual history with a story simple enough to support a predetermined political conclusion. Honest history serves neither conclusion. It serves only the record.

Smallpox blanket narratives are a case study in how the replacement story distorts the historical record it claims to be correcting. The claim, widely repeated in classrooms, documentaries, and political speeches, is that European colonizers systematically used smallpox-infected blankets as a weapon of biological genocide against Native American peoples. The historical record does not support that claim as stated.

There is one documented case of a deliberate attempt to spread smallpox through contaminated material. On June 24, 1763, during the siege of Fort Pitt in what is now

Pittsburgh, a fur trader and militia captain named William Trent gave two blankets and a handkerchief taken from the fort's smallpox ward to two Delaware emissaries following failed negotiations. Trent recorded it in his journal: we gave them two Blankets and an Handkerchief out of the Small Pox Hospital. An invoice submitted afterward to the British military for reimbursement confirms the account. General Jeffrey Amherst and his subordinate Colonel Henry Bouquet discussed the tactic in correspondence around the same time, with Amherst explicitly advocating it. The intent was clearly malicious. The documentation is real.

What is not documented is whether it worked. Historian Philip Ranlet, writing in Pennsylvania History in 2000, found no evidence that the scheme was effective. The smallpox epidemic in the Ohio Valley had already been underway before the June meeting, the tribes had recently had contact with the disease through other routes, and those already susceptible may have been infected before the blankets arrived. Smallpox spreads most efficiently through respiratory droplets during face-to-face contact, not through contact with contaminated objects, though blanket transmission is possible. Researchers cannot separate any effect of the blankets from the natural epidemic already spreading through the region. Historian Elizabeth Fenn, whose 2000 article in the Journal of American History is the most careful scholarly treatment of the episode, concluded that we simply cannot know whether the blankets contributed to the outbreak.

More important than the Fort Pitt episode is what the replacement narrative does with it. The one documented attempt at biological warfare by colonial forces, in 1763, by a British military garrison under siege, of uncertain effect, gets inflated in the replacement narrative into a systematic and deliberate policy of biological genocide applied across the continent and across centuries. The actual devastation of Native American populations by smallpox was real and catastrophic, estimates suggest the indigenous population of the Americas fell by as much as ninety percent following European contact.

But that devastation was overwhelmingly the product of natural spread, not deliberate infection. The first smallpox epidemics in the Americas began in 1519 with Spanish contact in Mexico, a century and a half before Fort Pitt, spreading through existing trade networks and population movements. The 1837 epidemic that reduced the Mandan tribe from approximately two thousand people to fewer than thirty survivors was spread by a fur company steamboat carrying infected passengers, a commercial failure of quarantine, not a deliberate act. The disease did not need to be weaponized. Its natural spread was catastrophic enough.

Honest history of what happened to Native American peoples during the centuries of European expansion does not require the blanket story to be true at the scale the replacement narrative claims. The land dispossession was real. The treaty violations were real. The deliberate destruction of cultures and forced removal of children to boarding schools were real and extensively documented. The actual record is damning enough without inflation. The inflation matters because when the historical record is made to support a conclusion it does not support, the people who notice the inflation use it to dismiss the real crimes along with the invented ones. The replacement narrative does not serve justice for what actually happened. It obscures it.

There is a deeper problem with the framework the replacement narrative uses to tell the story of European contact with the Americas, and it is worth naming directly. The replacement narrative treats European settlement of the Americas as a unique historical event in a category by itself, requiring a specific and permanent moral vocabulary that does not apply to comparable events elsewhere in human history. That treatment is not historical. It is political.

European settlement of the Americas was a large-scale migration of peoples into territory occupied by other peoples, accompanied by the displacement, death, and cultural transformation of those peoples over roughly four centuries. It was driven by the search for resources, land, and wealth, enabled by military and technological advantage, and accelerated by disease. The outcomes for the peoples who were already there were catastrophic. None of that is in dispute.

What is worth examining is how unique those outcomes were by the standards of human history. The Mongol conquests of the 13th century, under Genghis Khan and his successors, are estimated by historians to have killed between thirty and forty million people across Eurasia, roughly ten percent of the world's entire population at the time. Cities were depopulated. Entire agricultural regions were converted to steppe. China's recorded population fell by tens of millions. The Arab conquests of the 7th and 8th centuries swept across North Africa, displacing and eventually absorbing the indigenous Berber populations whose Christian communities ceased to exist entirely within a few centuries.

Arabic replaced Coptic, Latin, and Aramaic across vast regions that had spoken those languages for a thousand years. The Bantu migrations across sub-Saharan Africa over two thousand years displaced hundreds of populations across the continent. The Ottoman expansion transformed Anatolia demographically, displacing Greek and Armenian populations who had lived there for millennia. The Hun migrations of the 4th and 5th centuries destabilized the entire European continent, pushing peoples who in turn pushed others in cascading waves that contributed to the collapse of the Western Roman Empire. Before the Huns there were the earlier peoples they displaced, who had themselves displaced others.

None of these displacements are remembered in the same moral vocabulary that the replacement narrative applies exclusively to European settlement of the Americas. The Mongols are studied in history courses as extraordinary military strategists. The Arab conquests are taught as the spread of a great civilization. The Ottoman Empire is analyzed as a complex political system. The peoples displaced by these conquests are not the subject of land acknowledgments in university lecture halls. Their descendants are not offered reparations by the states that now occupy their former territories. The moral framework applied to European settlement in the Americas is not applied consistently to human history.

It is applied selectively, to one migration, by people whose political purpose is served by that selection. This is not an argument that the Mongols or the Arab conquerors or the Ottomans should be made to answer for their conquests in the same vocabulary the framework applies to the United States. The selective application to one case and not others is a political choice, not a historical one.

The selective application reveals something important. The replacement narrative's goal is not honest history. If it were, it would apply its framework consistently, and the catalogue of human displacement and conquest across all of history would require an accounting that no existing state or civilization could survive. Every people currently living somewhere is living where someone else used to live. The Angles and Saxons displaced the Celts who had displaced earlier peoples. The Arabs displaced the Berbers. The Bantu displaced the Khoisan. The Turks displaced the Anatolian Greeks. The pattern is universal. The decision to apply the moral framework exclusively to one case while exempting all others is a political choice, not a historical one.

Honest history of European settlement of the Americas holds the full record without selective inflation. The land dispossession was real and documented. The treaty violations were real and documented. The boarding school system was a legislated government policy whose effects persist in living communities. The deaths from disease, warfare, and displacement were catastrophic in scale. All of that is true and none of it requires the replacement narrative's selective framework to be documented or understood. The replacement narrative does not serve the people whose history it claims to tell. It serves the political project that deployed their history as a weapon.

What Was Actually Founded in 1776

The American founding was not a perfect event. People who held contradictions produced it, contradictions that should make any honest observer uncomfortable. Men who wrote that all men are created equal while owning other men. Men who articulated a theory of universal human rights while denying those rights to women, to the poor, and to the people whose land they were taking. The contradictions were not invisible to the founders themselves. They argued about them, agonized over them in some cases, and in other cases suppressed the argument because they could not resolve it and still hold the coalition together.

What they also produced, despite those contradictions, was something genuinely new in the history of human political organization. A written constitution that established limits on government power and protections for individual rights. A system of representative government accountable to the governed. A set of ideals, articulated in the Declaration of Independence, that became the standard against which the country's own failures could be measured and eventually corrected.

The abolitionist movement used the Declaration of Independence. Frederick Douglass used it. The civil rights movement used it. Martin Luther King used it. They did not use it despite its origins. They used it because its origins contained a genuine commitment to a principle that the country had not yet honored, and they held that commitment up against the reality and demanded that the country close the gap.

That is what the founding ideals produced over two centuries of American political life: a series of expansions of the original promise, achieved through political struggle, to include people who had been excluded from it. Women. Black Americans. Other excluded groups. The arc was not automatic and it was not fast and it cost people their lives. But the arc was real. And the framework that made the arc possible was the founding.

The villainization of the founding does not improve on that framework. It destroys the framework. A country whose founding is understood as a crime rather than an imperfect promise has no founding ideals to appeal to, no standard to hold itself accountable to, no shared story about what it is trying to become. It has only a crime, compounding.

The Curriculum and Its Consequences

By 2020, the reframing of American history as primarily a story of oppression had moved from universities to high schools to elementary schools. The 1619 Project curriculum was adopted by thousands of school districts. Critical race theory frameworks, initially developed for law schools, had migrated into K-12 teacher training programs and from there into classroom practice. The language of systemic racism, white privilege, and settler colonialism had become the standard vocabulary through which American history was being taught to children who were not yet old enough to evaluate the framework critically.

The consequences are measurable. Survey data from multiple civic literacy research organizations documents declining civic knowledge among young Americans, and the pattern is not random. The Annenberg Public Policy Center's annual Constitution Day survey, conducted every September since 2003, has documented that the percentage of Americans who can name all three branches of government has remained below 40 percent in most years, while the percentage who cannot name any branch has risen. The American Council of Trustees and Alumni's What Will They Learn? reports have documented since 2009 that most American colleges and universities have dropped required courses in American history and government while expanding requirements in identity-focused subjects. The decline is not uniform.

Young Americans know more about American failures than previous generations did. They know less about American achievements, American institutions, and the mechanisms of American self-governance. They can articulate the crimes of the founding with precision. They cannot, at comparable rates, articulate the principles of the Constitution or the mechanisms by which those principles have been enforced and extended.

It is not an accident of bad teaching. It is the predictable outcome of a curriculum designed to produce a specific kind of understanding. A young person who knows the crimes of American history in detail and the achievements of American history in outline is a young person who has been given a specific story about what the country is. That story does not produce civic engagement. It produces civic alienation. And civic alienation is precisely what America's adversaries identified as the target when they began applying their resources to the villainization project.

The founding was not a crime. It was a compromise with crimes that the principles it established eventually made untenable. That distinction is the difference between honest history and villainization. The curriculum that has taken hold in American schools has collapsed that distinction. What has been lost is not just historical accuracy. What has been lost is the shared story that allows a diverse people to believe they are engaged in a common project worth continuing.

I will say plainly what the villainization framework has made it professionally risky to say: America is the greatest country in the history of human civilization. Not perfect. Not without failures that are real and serious. But measured by the standard that matters, what it produced for the largest number of people over the longest period of time, no country comes close. The expansion of individual liberty. The protection of minority rights through law. The economic mobility that allowed generations of people who arrived with nothing to build something real. The military power that defeated fascism and held back Soviet expansion. The scientific and medical achievements that extended and improved human life across the planet. The openness to self-criticism that allowed the country to confront its worst failures and expand its founding promise to people it had excluded. No civilization in human history has done more of these things better. That is not nationalism. That is the historical record.

The Same Operation From the Other Direction

David Barton gave an estimated four hundred speeches a year. He advised the Texas State Board of Education. Glenn Beck called him the Library of Congress in shoes. His book about Thomas Jefferson was pulled by his own publisher after conservative Christian scholars documented what they called embarrassing factual errors and suspiciously selective quotations. The History News Network, whose readership is professional historians, voted it the least credible history book in print. None of that stopped his influence.

Christian nationalist revisionism is the mirror image of the 1619 Project. Where the 1619 Project argues that the American founding was a crime whose crimes define the country, Christian nationalist revisionism argues that the founding was a divine act whose Christian character defines the country. Both positions select their evidence to support a predetermined conclusion. Both positions have been criticized by credentialed scholars within their own ideological communities. Both positions are more useful as political mobilization tools than as honest history.

The most prominent architect of the Christian nationalist historical revision is David Barton, founder of a Texas-based organization called WallBuilders, which has spent more than three decades promoting the argument that the United States was founded as an explicitly Christian nation and that the separation of church and state is a modern myth invented by activist courts. Barton has no formal credentials in history, his only academic degree is a bachelor's in religious education from Oral Roberts University. He has nonetheless given an estimated four hundred speeches a year, partnered with Glenn Beck who called him the Library of Congress in shoes, advised the Texas State Board of Education on curriculum standards that affect textbooks used across the country, and built a homeschooling curriculum empire that has reached hundreds of thousands of students. He was named one of Time magazine's twenty-five most influential evangelicals.

Professional historians have systematically examined the record Barton relies on, including conservative evangelical historians who share Barton's faith but not his methods. In 2012 his book The Jefferson Lies, which argued that Thomas Jefferson was an orthodox Christian and that his support for church-state separation has been misrepresented, was pulled by Thomas Nelson, at the time the largest Christian publisher in the United States, after the publisher cited a loss of confidence in the book's factual accuracy. Secular critics did not lead the withdrawal.

Conservative scholars did it: Jay Richards of the Heritage Foundation and Warren Throckmorton and Michael Coulter of Grove City College, who documented what they described as embarrassing factual errors and suspiciously selective quotations. The History News Network, whose readership includes professional historians across the political spectrum, voted the book the least credible history book in print in 2012. John Fea of Messiah College, himself an evangelical, has written extensively that Barton selects any statement by a founder that is positive toward religion and uses it to demonstrate that all founders were Christians, making no distinction between generic religious language and orthodox Christian doctrine in particular.

Barton continued. His influence did not diminish after the retraction. He remains one of the most widely heard voices in American Christian education. The correction happened. It just did not matter to the audience that needed to hear it.

The historical documents do not support the Christian nation claim as Barton makes it. The Constitution contains no mention of Christianity, Jesus Christ, or any specific religion. Article Six explicitly prohibits religious tests for public office. The Virginia Act for Religious Freedom, drafted by Jefferson in 1779, was amended in the legislature to insert the phrase Jesus Christ, and the amendment was rejected by a substantial majority, a vote Jefferson noted in his autobiography as proof that the act was intended to protect people of every faith and none. James Madison's Memorial and Remonstrance Against Religious Assessments, written in 1785, is one of the most forceful arguments for church-state separation ever produced by an American statesman, written by the man who would become the principal architect of the Constitution.

Consider the Treaty of Tripoli, negotiated during Washington's administration, ratified unanimously by the Senate in 1797, and signed by John Adams, states in Article Eleven: the Government of the United States of America is not in any sense founded on the Christian religion. These are not obscure or contested documents. They are primary sources from the founding era, available to anyone who reads them without a predetermined conclusion to support.

Jefferson, Madison, Franklin, and Washington were Deists, not orthodox Christians in the theological sense. They believed in a creator and in Providence. They did not believe in the divinity of Christ, biblical inerrancy, or the necessity of revealed religion. Jefferson produced his own version of the Gospels by cutting out every supernatural element, leaving only the ethical teachings. Franklin expressed his doubts about the divinity of Jesus directly in correspondence. This does not diminish them. It accurately describes what they believed, which is what honest history requires.

Christian believers are not served by this revision, any more than the descendants of enslaved Americans are served by the 1619 Project. It serves the political project that deployed their history. Christians who want a civic culture shaped by their values are best served by honest arguments about what those values require, not by a falsified account of the founding that collapses under examination and gives critics of Christianity an easy target. The real founding, a diverse coalition of mostly Protestant Christians and Enlightenment Deists who agreed to build a government that protected religious liberty precisely because they could not agree on theology, is a more honest and more defensible foundation for that civic argument than a myth.

The book's argument is not that the villainization of America is a left-wing project. It is that honest American history is being replaced by politically motivated stories from multiple directions, and that the replacement serves political actors and foreign adversaries who benefit from a country that cannot agree on what it is. That argument requires naming both distortions, because the people who peddle them are united in their opposition to the honest version, even as they fight each other about which distortion to prefer.

My grandfather did not talk about the camp the way you might expect a man to talk about the worst thing that ever happened to him. He talked about it the way a man talks about something he has processed and decided not to be defined by. He was matter-of-fact. He had been through it. He had come out. He had a life. The details he shared were specific and he shared them without performance. The things he left out he left out deliberately, and I learned not to push.

What I understood, even as a child, was that he had survived something that required a reason to survive. Not the biological will to live, which is just animal. Something more specific than that. He believed the country he was fighting for was worth fighting for, and that belief carried him through three and a half years in conditions that killed men who had every biological reason to keep going. When he came home he did not wave that belief around. He just lived it. He built something. He raised a family. He was a Navy man and the son of a Navy man's world, and that world had a specific texture that I absorbed without knowing I was absorbing it.

This chapter makes me angrier than almost any other in this book. Not because the facts are worse than the facts in other chapters. Because it is personal. The story of men like my grandfather was taken and replaced with a story that would have made him unrecognizable to himself. I want to document exactly how that happened and who did it.

In 1971, John Kerry testified before the Senate Foreign Relations Committee about what American soldiers were doing in Vietnam. Kerry was a decorated veteran and he had organized Vietnam Veterans Against the War. His testimony was detailed, specific, and damning. He described atrocities he said soldiers had testified to:

systematic torture, the killing of civilians, the razing of villages. He used the phrase that would follow American veterans for a generation. He called them war criminals.

Kerry was not alone. The Vietnam era produced a sustained cultural campaign against the American military that went far beyond legitimate criticism of the war's conduct or strategy. It produced a cultural framework in which the American soldier was not a defender of the country but an instrument of its imperial violence, not someone making sacrifices in service of a genuine ideal but someone being used by the powerful to kill the powerless. That framework did not end with the war. It embedded itself in the cultural institutions that interpret American military service.

What followed over decades, the movies, the academic literature, the cultural assumptions that settled into the newsroom and the classroom, did not simply criticize specific wars or specific decisions. They produced a systematic reframing of the American military as an institution. The military was not an organization of citizens willing to sacrifice for others. It was a machine of empire, staffed by the poor and powerless who had no other options, deployed by the wealthy and connected in service of resource extraction and geopolitical domination. The individual soldier was either a victim of the system or a willing participant in its crimes. Neither framing left room for the simpler truth that most of the people who put on the uniform do so because they believe in something larger than themselves and are willing to die for it.

From Heroes to War Criminals: The Cultural Shift

The shift did not happen overnight. It accumulated across decades of cultural production, each element small enough to seem like ordinary criticism and the aggregate large enough to constitute a replacement story about what the military is.

Academic departments produced studies of militarism, imperialism, and the military-industrial complex that treated the existence of American military power as itself a form of aggression. The peace movement produced a cultural frame in which military service was at best a necessary evil and at worst a pathology, in which the soldier was defined by what they might do rather than what they actually did, in which the default assumption was suspicion rather than respect.

The news media adopted that frame. The coverage of American military operations from Vietnam forward systematically emphasized casualties, failures, and atrocities while treating success and sacrifice as either less newsworthy or as propaganda. The Abu Ghraib photographs received sustained front-page coverage for weeks. The individual acts of heroism that occurred in the same theater of operations during the same period received coverage proportional to their newsworthiness, which was determined by news organizations that had absorbed the frame in which American military action is primarily a story of harm.

Hollywood produced a generation of films in which the American military was either an incompetent bureaucracy, a machine of racial violence, or a tool of shadowy institutional interests. The films that celebrated military sacrifice and competence were produced too, and they were popular when they were released, which tells you something about what ordinary Americans believe about the people who serve. But the critical apparatus that shapes how culture is understood and taught dismissed those films as propaganda and elevated the films that confirmed the indictment as serious art.

The cumulative effect of this cultural production on the population of potential military recruits is not speculation. It is documented in the Pentagon's own research on declining propensity to serve among young Americans.

The percentage of young Americans who say they would consider military service has been declining for decades. The research on why consistently identifies a cultural factor: young people do not want to join an institution they have been taught to regard as morally compromised. The Abu Ghraib story illustrates the asymmetry directly.

Between May and September 2004, the New York Times ran more than fifty front-page stories on Abu Ghraib. In the same period, the Times ran three front-page stories on Medal of Honor recommendations from the same theater. Pew Research Center's annual State of the News Media reports have documented since 2004 that the dominant frame for American military coverage is casualty reporting, misconduct, and strategic failure, while coverage of unit performance, veteran outcomes, and institutional effectiveness is categorized as lower-news-value content.

Fifty. Count them. Then count the Medal of Honor stories.

What Veterans Actually Do

The man coaches youth football on Thursday evenings. He served two tours in Afghanistan and does not talk about either. His teams have won three championships. He sits on the water district board. He has not missed a local election in sixteen years.

Veterans vote at higher rates than non-veterans. They volunteer in their communities at higher rates. They run for office at higher rates. They start businesses at higher rates. They report higher rates of meaning and purpose in their lives, higher rates of civic engagement, and lower rates of the disconnection and anomie that characterize the population of non-veterans in the same age and demographic categories.

They came back and got more involved, not less. That pattern matters.

The data is not subtle. The culture ignores it anyway.

These are not the outcomes of a population that has been shaped by an institution built on violence and exploitation. These are the outcomes of a population that has been shaped by an institution that instilled a specific set of values: service, sacrifice, accountability, commitment to something larger than individual interest. Those values produce better citizens. The data is clear on this. The cultural frame that has replaced the data is not.

The veteran who comes home from two tours in Afghanistan, works a job, coaches youth sports, shows up to vote, and does not talk much about what he did is not a war criminal or a victim. He is a person who believed that what he did mattered, who paid a cost for that belief, and who has continued to invest in the community that sent him. There are millions of people like him. The cultural story being told about the military has made it progressively harder for young people to see themselves in that story rather than in the story of imperialism and exploitation.

The Strategic Value of Military Villainization

A military that cannot recruit cannot defend the country. That is a statement of arithmetic, not politics. The United States Army missed its recruiting goal by fifteen thousand soldiers in 2022, the worst shortfall since the establishment of the all-volunteer force in 1973. The Army's own research on why documented a cultural factor: eligible young men did not want to serve in an institution that the culture around them had defined as morally suspect.

Russia and China understand this. The Senate Intelligence Committee reports on Russian active measures document IRA operations designed to amplify anti-military sentiment in American social media, to promote narratives of veteran mistreatment and military incompetence, to seed content that associated military service with racism, violence, and institutional corruption. The Chinese government promotes military service and patriotism in its own youth content while serving American youth content that emphasizes the costs and moral compromises of military service.

The villainization of the American military is not solely the product of foreign actors. The domestic framework that produced it is real and was built by Americans for reasons that had nothing to do with Chinese or Russian strategic interests. But the domestic framework and the foreign amplification are compounding each other toward one strategic purpose: reducing the capacity of the United States to field a military that believes in what it is doing.

A military whose recruits have been taught that the institution they are joining is an instrument of oppression is not a military at the peak of its effectiveness. Morale, unit cohesion, and the willingness to accept risk in defense of something you believe in are not incidental to military effectiveness. They are central to it. The villainization of the military attacks all three. That is what makes it a national security problem rather than a cultural sensitivity complaint.

I have watched religion become less and less a part of people's lives over the course of my lifetime. Not dramatically, not all at once, but steadily. The churches that used to be full are less full. The institutions that held communities together, that fed people and cared for the sick and gave people a reason to show up for each other, are thinning out. And something specific moved in to fill the space they left. Not something better. Something that serves different interests entirely. That is what this chapter is about.

The communities I have lived in and worked in have changed in this regard. The social infrastructure that religious institutions once provided, the meals for people who needed them, the support for families in crisis, the framework for obligations to neighbors and strangers, has not been replaced by something equally durable. What has replaced it, in some cases, is the state, which does some of those things and does them badly. In other cases nothing has replaced it. The gap is visible if you know what to look for.

Something moved in to fill that space. Not something better. Something that answers to the state and serves the state's interests. I watched it happen in the communities I knew. I watch it still.

The United States was not founded as a theocracy. The Constitution prohibits the establishment of a state religion and protects the free exercise of religion from government interference. Both of those provisions matter and both of them have mattered throughout American history. The separation of church and state is a genuine achievement that protects both religious communities and non-religious ones from the imposition of others' beliefs through the power of government.

None of that is the target of the villainization campaign. The target is the role that religious institutions have played in producing and sustaining American civic life. The argument is not that religious communities should not be exempt from government regulation or that religious belief should not be subject to rational criticism. The argument is that religious institutions themselves are instruments of social control, that the values they transmit are mechanisms of oppression, and that the civic functions they perform should be replaced by secular alternatives operating under the authority of the state.

That argument has consequences. And they are measurable.

What Religious Institutions Actually Provided

When the pandemic closed the schools in 2020, it was churches across the country that organized food distribution to the families who had been eating school lunches. They did not apply for grants to do it. They did not submit demographic data. They opened their parking lots and loaded cars.

Religious institutions have been doing this for most of American history. Hospitals, schools, orphanages, food banks, housing for the homeless, care for the elderly, support for immigrants, recovery programs for the addicted, community for the isolated. The Catholic Church built the largest private school system in the history of the Western world. The historically Black churches were the institutional backbone of the civil rights movement. The evangelical network built hospitals in parts of the world that governments had abandoned.

These institutions did not do this work because the government told them to. They did it because their theology told them they had an obligation to the poor, the sick, and the stranger. That theology is a matter of religious conviction and not everyone shares it. But the social outcomes it produced were real and measurable and they served populations that the state, for all its resources, has consistently failed to serve as effectively.

Religious institutions also provided something harder to measure but equally important: a framework for meaning. They gave people a story about why suffering matters, why sacrifice is worth making, why the obligations of community are not just contractual but moral. They provided the intergenerational transmission of values that no government program has successfully replicated, the accountability of a community that knows you over time and holds you to standards that extend beyond the legal minimum, the experience of being part of something larger than individual gratification.

The decline of religious institutions in American life has been steady and measurable since the 1970s. The percentage of Americans who identify as religiously unaffiliated has risen from roughly five percent then to over thirty percent today. The speed of the decline accelerated in the 2000s and 2010s. And the social outcomes that tracked religious participation, including rates of charitable giving, volunteer work, social trust, and civic engagement, have declined along with it. These are not coincidences. They are the measurable consequences of the removal of institutions that performed specific social functions.

How Religion Became an Instrument of Oppression

The academic framework that produced the villainization of American religion did not begin with a claim that religion is false, though that claim is available in the secularist tradition. It began with a claim that is harder to argue against: that religion has been used to justify oppression. That claim is historically accurate. Slavery was defended with scripture. The subordination of women was justified by theology. The persecution of gay people was conducted in the name of God. These are real facts and they belong in honest accounts of both religion and American history.

Honest history does something different with those facts than the villainization framework does. Honest history says: these are ways that religious authority was misused, and they produced real harm, and communities of faith have wrestled with those failures and in many cases reformed in response to them. Villainization says: these are the natural products of what religion is, and therefore religion as a social force is an instrument of oppression whose influence should be minimized.

The second argument does not follow from the first. Every human institution has been used to justify oppression. The state has been used to justify oppression at a scale no religious institution has matched. The academy has justified oppression. Science has been weaponized in service of oppression. The conclusion that an institution whose authority has been misused should therefore be minimized would, applied consistently, require the minimization of every human institution that has ever existed. It is not applied consistently. It is applied to religion alone, and to Christianity in particular, in the American context.

The academic and media apparatus that has produced the systematic association of American Christianity with racism, patriarchy, and oppression has not applied comparable scrutiny to the secular ideologies that produced the twentieth century's greatest crimes. The Soviet Union was explicitly atheist. The Khmer Rouge was explicitly atheist. The Cultural Revolution was explicitly atheist. None of those facts appear in the curriculum that teaches American students that religion is the primary vehicle of oppression in human history.

The Strategic Dimension

A society organized around religious institutions is a society with distributed sources of moral authority that do not answer to the state. Churches, synagogues, mosques, and temples create horizontal bonds of community that operate outside the control of government and outside the reach of centralized narrative management. They transmit values across generations, and those values resist the ideological fashions of the moment. They provide a framework for evaluating the claims of political authority that does not depend on the state's own self-assessment.

This makes them resistant to the specific kind of ideological subversion that the villainization campaign is designed to produce. A person whose primary community is a religious congregation is harder to capture. Their framework for moral evaluation comes from a tradition that predates the current political moment by centuries or millennia. Their obligations extend upward to something transcendent rather than outward to an ideological movement. That is a different kind of anchor.

The Soviet targeting of religion as a strategic objective is not a claim that requires inference. It is documented in the Mitrokhin Archive. Christopher Andrew's analysis of the archive establishes that no institution dominated the attention of the Kremlin more than the Catholic Church and the state that directed it, the Holy See. Mitrokhin's own summary is direct: the anti-Soviet nature of the churches and the incompatibility of their beliefs with Marxist-Leninist ideology mandated that the organs of state security put a stop to their activities. The Vatican itself was identified as one of the main targets of observation and penetration by agents of the KGB.

They knew what they were doing. They documented it themselves.

What the archive documents is specific. The Moscow Patriarchate, Russia's official Orthodox church structure, was established in 1943 on Stalin's orders as an NKVD front organization, with key positions including bishops requiring approval from the KGB and the Communist Party's Ideological Department. Priests were used as agents of influence in the World Council of Churches and in front organizations including the Christian Peace Conference, created in 1958 to oppose the World Council of Churches and amplify Soviet positions inside Western religious communities. According to the archive, the future Russian Patriarch Alexius II worked for the KGB as agent DROZDOV and received an honorary citation for services rendered. KGB infiltration of the Catholic Church and Protestant denominations across the West is documented across multiple operations.

The strategy was not to destroy American religion directly, which was impossible. The strategy was to infiltrate it, fund its most divisive internal conflicts, amplify its critics, and associate its authority with the political positions most likely to produce backlash from the secular left. A church fighting internal battles over politics is a church not transmitting values. A church associated with one political faction is a church that has lost its capacity to serve as a unifying institution. Both outcomes served Soviet strategic interests. The archive documents operations designed to produce both outcomes.

Yuri Bezmenov, whose account of Soviet active measures this series has documented, was explicit about why undermining religion mattered as a component of ideological subversion. Undermine the transcendent framework that gives people reasons to resist, he said, and you make them more susceptible to the replacement framework you are trying to install. A person whose primary obligations extend to something the state cannot control is a person the state cannot fully capture. The systematic attack on American religious institutions was not incidental to the subversion project. It was central to it.

The domestic campaign against American religion did not require Soviet direction to produce this outcome. The academic framework arrived at the same destination through its own intellectual development. But the convergence of domestic anti-religious frameworks and foreign amplification of those frameworks has produced a measurable result: a population less embedded in religious community, less anchored in transcendent obligation, and more susceptible to the replacement story that the villainization campaign is offering.

You cannot destroy the institutions that produce civic virtue and then be surprised when civic virtue declines.

Chapter 4: Capitalism and Achievement

I have spent my career building things. Books, primarily, but books are a business like any other. You produce something, you find people who want it, you do the work, you repeat. Over more than a hundred books I have watched the professional world around me change in ways that the people inside those changes often could not see because they were too close to them.

The companies I worked with and around began absorbing the framework this book documents at different speeds through the 2010s. Not the ones I ran. The ones around me. The mandatory training programs. The demographic targets in hiring. The language that started appearing in corporate communications that had been academic language five years earlier and was now presented as professional common sense. I watched colleagues deal with it. I watched some of them embrace it and some of them quietly maneuver around it and some of them leave.

What I noticed most was what happened to the people who built things. Not the administrators of things. The builders. The ones who showed up early and stayed late and produced results and expected to be judged on results. The framework had no place for them. It had a vocabulary for privilege and systemic advantage and the unearned nature of success, and that vocabulary did not fit the people I was watching. The special forces veterans I hired as consultants especially. Men who had earned everything they had through sustained effort against real resistance, in conditions that do not permit self-delusion. The framework that says achievement is primarily a function of unearned advantage had clearly never met any of them. And the people running the framework were not interested in meeting them. That was the tell.

The United States produced, in the century and a half following the Civil War, the greatest expansion of material well-being in human history. Not for everyone equally and not without costs that were real and are worth examining honestly. But the aggregate achievement was extraordinary: a country that went from a largely agricultural economy to the dominant industrial and technological power on earth, that lifted more people out of poverty than any other society in history, that produced innovations in medicine, communication, transportation, and information technology that transformed how human beings live everywhere on the planet.

A specific economic system produced that achievement, within a specific legal and political framework. It was not the product of central planning. It was not the product of state direction. It was the product of decentralized decision-making by millions of people and organizations competing, failing, adapting, and occasionally succeeding in ways that produced outcomes nobody planned and nobody could have planned. That system is called capitalism. It is the target.

The academic framework that has produced the villainization of American capitalism does not dispute the productivity data. It disputes the conclusion that should be drawn from the productivity data. The argument is not that capitalism failed to produce wealth. The argument is that the wealth it produced was stolen, that the system that produced it operates through exploitation rather than exchange, and that the achievement should be understood primarily through the lens of who it harmed rather than who it benefited.

The 1619 Economics

Beyond history, the 1619 Project extended its argument into economics. The lead economic essay argued that the wealth of the United States was built primarily on slavery and that contemporary American capitalism is best understood as the continuation of that foundation. The argument drew on the work of a school of historians who call themselves the New History of Capitalism, which emphasizes the connections between slave labor and industrial development in the nineteenth century.

Some of those connections are real. Cotton picked by enslaved people was the primary raw material for the textile mills of New England and Britain. The financial instruments that funded American industrial development were connected to the plantation economy. These facts belong in honest accounts of American economic history.

The conclusion drawn from them, that contemporary American capitalism is therefore slavery by other means, does not follow from the historical evidence. American capitalism in 2026 is not the cotton economy of 1845. The legal framework is different. The labor force is free. The institutional protections against exploitation, however imperfect, exist and have teeth. The economy that produced the iPhone and the COVID vaccine and the logistics infrastructure that fed the world during a pandemic is not the same economy that produced the plantation. Treating them as continuous expressions of the same fundamental structure is not historical analysis. It is a political argument dressed in historical clothes.

The Villainization of Achievement

More consequential than the attack on the economic system itself is the attack on individual achievement as a cultural value. The argument that capitalism is exploitation requires, as a supplement, the argument that individual success within a capitalist system is either a function of exploitation or a function of unearned advantage. The concept of privilege, as deployed in contemporary institutional settings, performs this function.

The privilege framework does not say that individual achievement is impossible. It says that individual achievement is always conditioned by systemic factors that advantaged some people before they made a single decision about their own lives. That observation contains a grain of truth: it is easier to succeed if you were born into a family with resources, social capital, and access to good schools. Nobody serious disputes that. What the privilege framework does with that grain of truth is different from what honest analysis does with it.

Honest analysis says: advantages and disadvantages at birth condition but do not determine outcomes, and a fair society should work to reduce those advantages and disadvantages while still rewarding effort and talent. The privilege framework says: advantages and disadvantages at birth so thoroughly determine outcomes that individual effort and talent are secondary factors, and therefore individual success is best understood as a function of privilege rather than merit.

That argument, applied consistently, produces a specific kind of social outcome. It discourages the belief that individual effort matters, because if outcomes are determined by systemic forces, effort is either irrelevant or morally suspect as an explanation for differential outcomes. It discourages the aspiration to achieve, because achievement becomes evidence of unearned advantage rather than earned success. It produces, in the people who fully absorb it, a disposition toward passivity and grievance rather than agency and aspiration.

The data on this is not subtle. Raj Chetty's Opportunity Atlas, the largest study of economic mobility ever conducted in the United States, tracked the economic outcomes of thirty million Americans over decades and documented that mobility rates vary enormously across communities, ranging from the lowest in some urban counties to rates comparable to Denmark in others, often within the same metropolitan area. The variation is not primarily explained by race or class at birth.

Community-level factors explain it: family structure, civic participation, school quality, and the presence of institutions that transmit the values associated with economic effort. The countries and communities that maintain strong beliefs in the connection between individual effort and outcomes show higher rates of economic mobility. The communities that have absorbed the framework in which outcomes are primarily determined by systemic forces show the reverse, which is the expected outcome when the framework successfully convinces people that effort is futile. The framework is not just wrong as economics. It is damaging as psychology.

Who the Villainization of Capitalism Serves

That framework does not serve the people at the bottom of the economic ladder. The historical evidence on this is clear: the periods of greatest economic mobility for poor Americans have been the periods when economic growth was strongest, when the belief in individual opportunity was most widely shared, and when the institutions that transmitted the skills and values required for economic participation, schools, families, religious communities, were most functional.

The message to poor Americans is that the system is rigged and their only recourse is political organization against it. That message is not without some truth. The system does have structural features that disadvantage some people. But the message that the system is so thoroughly rigged that individual effort cannot move the needle is demonstrably false. Millions of people have moved from poverty to middle-class stability through exactly the combination of effort, education, and community that the framework dismisses as naive.

What it serves is the professional class that has built careers on the premise that the system cannot be fixed from within by people making better decisions, but only from above by experts applying the correct frameworks. It serves a class of administrators, consultants, advocates, and academics whose professional existence depends on the persistence of the problems they claim to be addressing. A poor community that successfully organizes itself to transmit the values and skills required for economic participation does not need the services of the DEI apparatus. A poor community that has been taught that individual effort is futile and systemic change is the only path forward will reliably need those services forever. The industry that delivers that message has no financial interest in disproving it.

Chapter 5: The Symbols

I grew up in California. I no longer live there. One of the things I noticed, long before I left, was what happened to the flag. Not the formal moments with the flag, the funerals and the ceremonies, those held on longer. The informal ones. The flags on porches. The flags on trucks. The flags that people put up just because they felt like it. In the California of my childhood those were common enough that they did not require explanation. In the California I left they had become a statement, which is a different thing entirely. A statement about what you believe. A signal about which side you are on. The same piece of cloth, in the same geography, had become politically charged in ways it never used to be.

That shift did not happen by accident. I did not understand at the time what had produced it. I understand now. What happened to the flag in California is what has been happening to American symbols broadly, and the mechanism that produced it is the mechanism this book is tracing through every other domain it has touched.

Symbols are not decorations. They are the compressed form of a story. When a soldier folds a flag and hands it to a widow, both of them know, without saying it, what the flag means in that moment: that someone believed in something enough to die for it, and that the country they defended recognizes the cost. When a crowd stands for the national anthem before a game, something happens in the room that is not just social ritual. It is the brief, collective acknowledgment that these people, however different they are in every other way, are part of the same story.

Destroy the symbols and you do not destroy the story. You make the story harder to access. You remove the compressed form and replace it with nothing, or with a counter-story in which the symbol represents not a shared aspiration but a shared crime. And when enough people have absorbed the counter-story, the moment of collective acknowledgment does not happen anymore. The crowd stands or sits or turns away based on individual calculation about political alignment, and the brief unity that the symbol made possible is gone.

This is what the villainization of American symbols is designed to produce. Not the destruction of the flag or the anthem or the monuments, though that has happened in some cases. The destruction of what the symbols do when they work.

The Flag

In 2012, Clint Eastwood brought an empty chair to the Republican National Convention to represent Barack Obama. In 2016, Colin Kaepernick knelt during the national anthem. Two symbolic acts, opposite political registers, both instantly understood by everyone who saw them, because the flag and the anthem carry enough shared meaning to be argued over. That is what a living national symbol looks like. The argument about what it means is not the problem. The problem is when enough people conclude that it means nothing worth arguing about.

Over decades of deliberate cultural production, the flag accumulated a different set of associations. In the cultural space occupied by the academic and media apparatus, something closer to: the crimes of the founding, the violence of the military, the oppression of minorities, and the arrogance of a nation that believes itself exceptional. These associations are not random. They were built, deliberately, through decades of cultural production that consistently associated the flag with the worst chapters of American history and consistently avoided associating it with the best chapters.

The consequence is measurable. Survey data shows that pride in American nationality has been declining, most sharply among young Americans and most sharply among the college-educated. The percentage of Americans who say they are extremely proud to be American fell from fifty-five percent in 2001 to thirty-nine percent in 2023, the lowest number ever recorded. Among Americans under thirty, the number is lower still. The flag that once united across political lines now divides along them. Whether you display it has become a political statement, which means it has partially stopped being a national symbol and started being a tribal one.

The Monuments

The removal of monuments to Confederate leaders was, in many cases, a legitimate response to the placement of those monuments in positions of civic honor in the first place. Robert E. Lee led an army against the United States in defense of slavery. His statue does not belong in a place of civic honor in a courthouse or a capitol building. That is a defensible position and the argument for it does not require the villainization framework to sustain it.

What the monument removal movement became is something different. The statues of Confederate generals came down and kept coming. Christopher Columbus came down. Thomas Jefferson came down. Abraham Lincoln came down, in Portland and in San Francisco, on the grounds that his policies toward Native Americans were insufficiently progressive by contemporary standards. The monument to the 54th Massachusetts Infantry, the Black Civil War regiment memorialized in the film Glory, was vandalized. The logic of the framework, once applied, found no natural stopping point, because the framework's standard is not whether a historical figure held the best available views of their time but whether they held views acceptable by the standards of the present moment.

No historical figure passes that test consistently. The standard, applied rigorously, produces the conclusion that American history contains no figures worth honoring, which is the conclusion that serves the villainization project's purposes. A country whose history contains no honorable figures is a country whose past is entirely a source of shame and whose story provides no material for the construction of a shared identity worth defending.

What Symbols Do and What Happens Without Them

The literature on symbols and social cohesion is not subtle. Émile Durkheim's foundational sociology identified shared ritual and symbol as the mechanism by which societies maintain the collective identity required for cooperation at scale. Robert Bellah's concept of American civil religion, developed across decades of scholarship beginning in 1967, documented how the flag, the anthem, and the monuments function as the ritual infrastructure of American civic life, carrying a shared moral vocabulary that transcends religious and political differences. Robert Putnam's research on social capital documented that communities with stronger shared symbolic and civic participation showed higher rates of trust, lower crime, and better economic outcomes. Shared symbols are not aesthetic choices. They are the infrastructure of a shared story, the visible form of the claim that these people, however different in every other dimension, are engaged in a common project.

Remove that infrastructure and the common project does not automatically reconstitute itself in a different form. What research on social cohesion consistently finds is that the removal of shared symbolic frameworks produces fragmentation, tribalism, and the retreat into smaller, more exclusive identity groups that provide the sense of belonging the national framework no longer provides. The country does not become a community of free people with no symbolic obligations. It becomes a collection of competing tribes whose primary loyalty is to their own group and whose relationship to the wider polity is transactional at best and hostile at worst.

The observation is sociological, not ideological. When the symbolic infrastructure of collective identity is dismantled faster than replacement infrastructure can be built, fragmentation follows. The villainization of American symbols has dismantled that infrastructure, in the educational system, in the media, and in the cultural space where the next generation forms its understanding of what it is part of. Nothing has been built to replace it. The result is visible in the data on civic participation, institutional trust, social isolation, and the declining propensity to serve in the military.

A country that cannot agree on what its symbols mean cannot agree on much else. And a country that cannot agree on much else is a country that its adversaries can exploit.

You do not have to love everything a symbol has meant to understand that the symbol's destruction leaves something broken that cannot easily be replaced.

Chapter 6: The Land – What the Bison Story Gets Wrong

The bison chapter makes me angry in a specific way. The factual argument, the actual ecological history, is so much more interesting and useful than the replacement story. It is the kind of complicated truth that teaches future generations how to think about land, about species, about what actually happens when two worlds collide. The simple version throws that away. And I think it does it partly out of ignorance, because the original framework was built before the Columbian Exchange was understood well enough to complicate the narrative. They were not lying. They just did not know what we know now. They built a story on an incomplete record and then refused to update it when the record got fuller.

The villainization of America does not stop at its history, its institutions, or its people. It extends to the country's relationship with the land itself. The ecological narrative that has taken hold in American education and media tells a specific story about American environmental history: that European settlers arrived, systematically destroyed the natural world through greed and deliberate policy, and that the near-extinction of the American bison, the most iconic ecological catastrophe on the continent, is the defining example of what white settlement did to the American landscape. The story is taught as settled. It is not settled. It is a partial truth that, like the other partial truths this book examines, obscures more than it reveals and serves political purposes more than it serves the land.

The Simple Story

The simple story goes like this. Before Europeans arrived, 30 to 60 million bison roamed the Great Plains in herds so vast that eyewitness accounts described them as stretching to the horizon in every direction. Native Americans lived in balance with these herds, taking what they needed and no more, maintaining a sustainable ecological relationship that had persisted for thousands of years. Then white settlers arrived, commercial hunters followed, and within a few decades of industrialized slaughter the bison were gone, reduced from tens of millions to fewer than a thousand animals by 1889. The US Army encouraged and participated in the slaughter to destroy the food supply of Plains Indian nations and break their resistance to forced relocation. The ecological catastrophe was deliberate, the instrument of a colonial policy designed to eliminate both the animal and the culture that depended on it.

Parts of this story are true and documented. The commercial hide hunt of the 1870s and 1880s was real and devastating. At the peak of the market, a single bison hide fetched three dollars in eastern cities, equivalent to roughly fifty dollars today, and hundreds of professional hunters with high-powered Sharps rifles moved across the plains in systematic sweeps. The southern herd was commercially extinct by 1880. The northern herd followed by 1885. By 1889 the US Biological Survey counted 541 wild bison remaining on the continent. General Philip Sheridan told the Texas legislature in 1875 that the hide hunters deserved medals rather than censure, because destroying the bison would do more to end the Indian problem than the entire US Army combined. The intent to use the slaughter as a weapon of displacement was explicit and documented. None of this is invention.

But it is not the complete story. It erases a biological transformation that began a century and a half before the commercial hunters arrived, makes the ecological catastrophe simpler than it was, and in doing so prevents understanding the full chain of causation that connects the bison's near-extinction to one of the worst ecological disasters in American history. That disaster, the Dust Bowl of the 1930s, devastated white farmers as thoroughly as the hide hunters had devastated the Plains Indians. The honest ecological history does not serve a clean villain narrative. It serves something more important: an accurate account of what was lost, and why.

The Columbian Exchange and the Horse

What actually happened on the Great Plains began a century and a half earlier, not in the 1870s with commercial hunters. It began in 1519, when Hernán Cortés landed on the Gulf Coast of Mexico with sixteen horses, the first horses on the North American continent since the Pleistocene extinction roughly ten thousand years earlier. The horse was a European import, one component of what historian Alfred Crosby called the Columbian Exchange: the vast, mostly unintentional transfer of plants, animals, and pathogens between the Old and New Worlds that began with Columbus and transformed both hemispheres permanently.

Horses spread north through indigenous trade networks faster than European settlement followed. The Pueblo Revolt of 1680, in which the Pueblo people of New Mexico drove the Spanish out of the region and captured their horse herds, accelerated the process dramatically. By 1700 horses had reached the northern Plains. By the 1730s the Comanche had mastered equestrian culture with a speed that astonished contemporary observers, transforming themselves within a generation from a pedestrian people of the Rocky Mountain foothills into the dominant military and commercial power of the southern Plains. By the time of the French and Indian War in the 1760s, the mounted Plains warrior, equipped with both horses from Spanish trade routes and guns from French and British ones, was a formidable military presence across the entire central continent.

Everything changed with the horse. Tribes that had hunted bison on foot, using cliff drives and coordinated chases, could now pursue individual animals across open ground at speed. Kill rates increased dramatically. Trade networks that had previously moved bison products in limited quantities now moved them at scale. The Comanche built a commercial empire that stretched from the northern Plains into Mexico, with bison hides and horses as its primary commodities. The Cheyenne and Arapaho entered intensive robe production in the 1820s to supply the American fur trade. What had been subsistence hunting with selective pressure became something closer to commercial hunting under different management.

Decades before the first professional hide hunters appeared, the ecological damage was already building. Historian Pekka Hämäläinen, whose scholarship on the Comanche is among the most thorough in American historical literature, documents what happened: the large horse herds required to sustain the equestrian economy competed with bison for the limited riverine resources that both species depended on for winter survival. The deep river valleys of the southern Plains, the cottonwood groves along the Cimarron, the Arkansas, the Canadian, were the only places horses could find winter forage.

Bison relied on the same valleys for winter shelter. As domestic horse herds grew into the millions across the southern Plains, the competition for these critical winter resources intensified. The Encyclopedia of the Great Plains documents that by the early 1840s the river valleys had already become overexploited, pushing bison herds into a decline that predated the commercial hunt by thirty years. On the southern Plains, bison herds were already seriously depleted by the 1830s from the combined pressure of horse competition, commercial robe trading, and drought cycles, before a single professional hide hunter had arrived.

This is not an argument that Plains Indians caused the bison's decline. It is an argument that the horse, a European import, itself part of the Columbian Exchange, transformed the ecological dynamics of the Plains in ways that began straining the bison population long before the commercial market delivered the final blow. The chain of causation is longer and more complex than the simple story allows.

The Commercial Hunt and Its Architects

When the commercial hide hunters came in the 1870s and 1880s, they finished what had already begun. The Army's role in encouraging them was as deliberate as the documentary record shows. The hide market was driven by eastern demand for industrial leather belting, the primary industrial use of bison hide at the time, as well as robes and rugs. The railroads made the slaughter economically viable by providing transportation for hides to eastern markets and supplying hunters with a base of operations. The kill rate at peak operation was staggering: some estimates place it at several thousand animals per day across the plains. The southern herd of perhaps 20 million animals was commercially extinct within roughly a decade. The scale and speed have no parallel in documented ecological history.

General Sheridan's statement to the Texas legislature was not passive approval. It was explicit policy. to the Texas legislature, that the hide hunters should be given medals for doing more to solve the Indian problem than the Army could, was not an offhand remark. The policy logic was explicit: destroy the bison, destroy the food supply, break the resistance, force the relocation. Congress twice considered bills to protect bison herds. Both times Sheridan lobbied against them and both times they failed. The deliberate weaponization of ecological destruction against a civilian population is documented and belongs in any honest accounting of what happened.

What the simple story leaves out is the multi-factor nature of the collapse. Disease was a contributing factor, cattle introduced bovine diseases to which bison had no immunity, and outbreaks swept through herds already under commercial hunting pressure. Competition from the cattle industry itself, which moved onto the Plains immediately behind the hide hunters, displaced bison from remaining range. And crucially, the smallpox epidemics that had been killing Plains Indians since the eighteenth century had, paradoxically, temporarily allowed bison populations to expand by reducing human hunting pressure, creating an artificially elevated baseline that made the eventual collapse look steeper than the long-term equilibrium would have been.

What Was Actually Lost: The Bison as Keystone

The honest ecological history of bison loss requires understanding what bison actually were, not just a food source for Plains Indians and a commercial resource for hide hunters, but a keystone species whose grazing behavior had maintained the entire prairie ecosystem for ten thousand years.

Keystone species are those whose presence affects an ecosystem out of all proportion to their biomass, remove them and the system does not merely shrink; it reorganizes from the ground up. Bison were keystone grazers of the Great Plains in precisely this sense.

Their grazing was selective and rotational: they grazed intensively in one area, then moved, allowing deep-rooted native grasses to recover. Their wallowing, rolling in bare soil to shed parasites, created hundreds of thousands of shallow depressions across the prairie that collected water and created habitat for dozens of dependent species. Their migration patterns distributed nutrient cycling across enormous areas. Their hooves, moving in massive herds, aerated the soil rather than compacting it. The deep-rooted native grasses that coevolved with bison grazing developed root systems extending six to twelve feet into the soil, anchoring topsoil, retaining moisture, and maintaining the soil structure of the prairie under conditions that would have eroded more fragile systems.

Decades of experimental research at the Konza Prairie Biological Station in Kansas, where bison have been reintroduced to tallgrass prairie, has documented continued increases in native plant species richness and resilience to drought compared to ungrazed and cattle-grazed plots. The difference between bison and cattle as grazers is not merely cultural sentiment about native species. It is a documented ecological difference in how their grazing patterns, movement, and behavior interact with the prairie system they coevolved with.

When the bison were gone, the prairie ecosystem lost its keystone. The deep-rooted native grasses that bison grazing maintained were the first casualty, replaced by the shallow-rooted annual crops that settlers plowed the plains to plant. A hundred million acres of native prairie grassland were converted to wheat and corn agriculture between the 1870s and the 1920s, land that had held its topsoil through drought and wind for millennia, held by grass root systems that extended further into the earth than the crops that replaced them reached above it. The US Department of the Interior's own documentation of the bison restoration program states it directly: the persecution of bison contributed to the decline of healthy grassland ecosystems and, eventually, to the Dust Bowl in the 1930s.

The Dust Bowl and Its True Cause

The Dust Bowl of the 1930s is remembered as a natural disaster, a drought that turned the Great Plains to dust. The drought was real. What is less commonly understood is that the vulnerability was built, over decades, through an ecological transformation that began with the removal of the bison and continued with the plowing of the prairie they had maintained.

When the drought struck in waves across the 1930s, 1934, 1936, 1939, it did not find the deep-rooted, self-stabilizing prairie that had existed a century earlier. It found 100 million acres of plowed cropland with shallow-rooted annual crops whose root systems had no capacity to hold the topsoil against wind. The native grasses that had anchored that soil through drought cycles for thousands of years were gone. The bison whose grazing had maintained those grasses were gone. The soil structure that both had maintained together was degraded by two generations of industrial agriculture conducted on land that was never ecologically suited to it, on crops that had replaced the ecosystem that had made the soil in the first place.

The result was the worst man-made ecological disaster in American history. In many regions of the High Plains, more than seventy-five percent of the topsoil was blown away by the end of the 1930s. Three and a half million people were displaced from the southern Plains. The per-acre value of farmland in high-erosion counties declined by nearly thirty percent and never fully recovered. John Steinbeck documented the human cost in The Grapes of Wrath. What Steinbeck did not document, because it was not yet understood, was the chain of ecological causation that connected the hide hunters of the 1870s to the dust storms of the 1930s through the removal of a keystone species and the destruction of the ecosystem it had maintained.

The people who suffered most from the Dust Bowl were not Native Americans. They were white settlers, the descendants of homesteaders who had moved onto the plains after the bison were gone, plowed land that should never have been plowed, and paid the ecological price of an agricultural system built on the ruins of the one that had preceded it. The villain narrative of the bison story, white settlers destroyed the bison as an act of deliberate ecological genocide, does not account for this outcome. It does not explain why the people who benefited from the bison's destruction also suffered, catastrophically, from the ecological consequences of that destruction. Honest ecological history does.

What Honest History Requires

Honest history of the American bison holds all of it: the Columbian Exchange that introduced the horse and transformed Plains ecology before European settlement was complete; the Native American commercial hunting that intensified under the horse culture and created ecological strain decades before the hide hunters arrived; the commercial slaughter of the 1870s and 1880s, which was the proximate cause of near-extinction and was consciously weaponized as a tool of displacement; the Army's documented policy of using ecological destruction against civilian populations; the loss of a keystone species whose ecological function maintained the entire prairie system; and the downstream consequence, the Dust Bowl, that destroyed the people who had benefited from the destruction as thoroughly as the destruction had destroyed its intended targets.

A simple villain narrative does not serve the land. It produces a story in which ecological destruction is understood as the product of white malice, which means the lesson it teaches is moral rather than ecological. A generation educated in the simple narrative learns that the bison were destroyed because of who destroyed them, not because of what was destroyed and what the destruction set in motion. That lesson produces no useful guidance about how to manage land, how to maintain keystone species, or how to avoid the agricultural errors that turned a continent's prairie into a dust bowl.

The honest ecological history produces different lessons. It documents that ecosystems maintained over thousands of years by keystone species cannot be disrupted without cascading consequences that may take generations to manifest. It documents that agricultural systems imposed on land without understanding the ecological system they are replacing will eventually fail on that land's own terms. It documents that the destruction of a species is not merely a moral event but an ecological one whose consequences extend far beyond the immediate act. These are lessons the land is still teaching. The simple story cannot hear them, because the simple story is not listening to the land. It is listening to the argument.

Bison did not disappear because of who killed them. They disappeared because of what they were. What was lost was larger than the animal.

Part Two: The Internal Architects

The domestic institutions that built the villainization framework and the incentive structures that keep it running.

Chapter 7: The Academy

When I wrote The Enshittification of America I felt the same thing I feel writing this chapter: sadness. Something good had been corrupted. The university is supposed to be the place where honest inquiry happens, where ideas get tested against evidence, where the best argument wins regardless of who made it. Watching that get hollowed out by people who either do not mean well or who are, in some cases, genuinely hostile to what the institution was built to do, that is not a political observation. It is a grief observation. Something worth preserving was not preserved.

In 1987, Allan Bloom published The Closing of the American Mind. He was dismissed as a reactionary. He was not wrong. What he documented in 1987 has become, in the four decades since, not a warning but a description. The system finished the transformation he was watching begin.

The specific operation was: replace the principle that a common body of knowledge exists and that claims about it can be evaluated by consistent standards with the claim that knowledge is produced by and serves the interests of specific social groups, and that the relevant question about any claim is not whether it is true but whose interests it serves. That replacement did not happen in one decisive moment. It happened over four decades of hiring, curriculum revision, accreditation pressure, and the simple mechanism of ensuring that the people who would have argued against it were not in the room. The result is the institution the rest of this chapter documents.

The Long March Through History

The specific application of critical theory to American history produced a body of academic literature, beginning in earnest in the 1970s and accelerating through the 1980s and 1990s, that systematically reinterpreted every major chapter of American history through the lens of race, class, and gender. The founding became a story about property-owning white men protecting their interests. The westward expansion became a story of genocide. The industrial revolution became a story of labor exploitation. The New Deal became a story of racial exclusion. World War II became, in some versions, a story of American racism and empire alongside the more familiar story of fascism defeated.

None of these interpretations is entirely false. All of them contain insights that honest history should incorporate. What they do collectively, when they become the dominant framework rather than one perspective among several, is replace a complicated story with a simple one: American history is primarily the history of oppression, and every chapter of it, viewed through the correct lens, confirms that conclusion.

That story reached the textbooks through a specific institutional mechanism that is worth tracing in detail. Paulo Freire's Pedagogy of the Oppressed, published in 1968 by a Brazilian educator and originally developed for adult literacy programs in the developing world, was adopted by Teachers College at Columbia University, which sits immediately adjacent to the original home of the Frankfurt School in New York. Teachers College became the primary disseminator of what became called critical pedagogy, the application of Freire's framework to American K-12 education. The framework holds that traditional education is a form of oppression, that teachers should help students develop critical consciousness about the systems that oppress them, and that the curriculum is a site of political contestation rather than a body of knowledge to be transmitted. By the 1990s, Pedagogy of the Oppressed was among the most assigned texts in American education schools.

A study by the National Association of Scholars documented it as one of the most frequently required books in teacher preparation programs nationally. The teachers certified by education schools trained in this framework carried it into classrooms across the country. The people who write and review educational standards, who design curricula, and who certify teachers had all been processed through institutions where the framework was not one perspective among several but the professional consensus.

The Strategy Behind the March

The capture of American universities was not an accident of intellectual fashion. It was the execution of a strategy that had been articulated in published documents for decades before it reached American institutions. Antonio Gramsci, the Italian Marxist theorist who wrote in a Fascist prison in the 1930s, had argued that the reason socialist revolution had failed in the industrialized West was not the failure of the working class but the failure of the intellectual class. The workers were held in place not primarily by violence but by cultural hegemony, the set of assumptions, values, and common sense that the ruling class had embedded in the institutions of civil society: schools, churches, newspapers, voluntary associations. Change the culture and you change the political order. To change the culture, capture the institutions.

Gramsci died before his theory could be tested at scale. It was tested by a generation of activists in the 1960s and 1970s who had absorbed his argument and applied it to American conditions. The German student radical Rudi Dutschke coined the phrase that became the movement's operational doctrine: the long march through the institutions. Not a frontal assault on the state. A generational occupation of the schools, the media, the foundations, the professional associations, and the regulatory agencies. Take the positions. Train the successors. Wait.

Herbert Marcuse, the Frankfurt School philosopher who taught at Brandeis and UC San Diego and whose work One-Dimensional Man became essential reading for the American New Left, translated Gramsci's institutional strategy into an argument aimed directly at American universities. Marcuse argued that the university was the critical institution because it produced the professional class that would go on to staff every other institution. Capture the university and you capture the pipeline to everything else. His students included Angela Davis. His influence on the generation of academics who shaped American humanities and social sciences in the 1970s and 1980s is documented and direct.

None of this required a conspiracy. What Gramsci and Marcuse provided was a theory, openly published and widely discussed, that explained to a generation of left-wing intellectuals why they should pursue academic careers rather than electoral politics. The long march through the institutions is not a secret operation. It is the explicit strategic framework of a documented political tradition. The outcomes documented in the rest of this chapter are not the unintended consequences of normal institutional drift. They are the intended outcomes of a deliberate strategy, pursued with discipline and patience across half a century.

An intellectual framework that cannot be challenged from within the institution is not scholarship. It is a religion with a university budget.

The Production of a Specific Kind of Graduate

The modern American university, in its humanities and social sciences departments, produces graduates with a specific intellectual profile. They can identify instances of racism, sexism, colonialism, and exploitation across time and geography with precision and confidence. They understand the mechanisms of power and the ways that language and symbol can serve the interests of the powerful while appearing neutral. They are trained in the epistemology of standpoint, the claim that what you can know is shaped by who you are, and they apply this framework consistently to the claims of anyone they identify as speaking from a position of dominance.

What they are frequently not trained in is the epistemology that evaluates claims by their evidence rather than by the identity of the person making them. They are not trained in the history of the ideas they are applying, which would allow them to understand those ideas as products of specific historical moments rather than timeless truths. They are not trained in the achievements of the civilization they are critiquing, which would give them a more complete picture of what they are evaluating. And they are not trained in the alternatives to the arrangements they critique, which would allow them to ask whether the alternatives are better or only different.

This is not a universal description of every college graduate. It is a description of a specific intellectual disposition that the humanities and social sciences, as currently organized, systematically produce. FIRE's 2021 College Free Speech Rankings surveyed 37,000 students at 159 colleges and found that more than 80 percent of students reported self-censoring at least occasionally, and that this rate was highest at the most prestigious institutions. Greg Lukianoff and Jonathan Haidt's The Coddling of the American Mind (2018) documented in detail how the intellectual norms instilled by American higher education had shifted in ways that discouraged the tolerance for disagreement that honest inquiry requires.

Those graduates go on to run the institutions that determine how American public life is interpreted: the newsrooms, the HR departments, the publishing houses, the NGOs, the government agencies that set educational standards. The framework they carry with them does not stay in the seminar room. It becomes the operating assumption of the institutions they enter.

Ask one of these graduates whether they consider themselves to be implementing an ideological program. Most will say no. They will say they are applying evidence-based practices, following professional standards, centering marginalized voices. The framework does not feel like a framework to people inside it. It feels like common sense. That is the point at which any framework becomes genuinely powerful.

The Ratio and Its Consequences

Ten to one. That is the ratio of Democratic to Republican faculty in American humanities and social science departments, from Mitchell Langbert's 2018 study of elite liberal arts colleges, published in Academic Questions. Without the two military academies, it was 12.7 to one. History departments: 33.5 to one. Sociology and anthropology, in some institutions: between 40 and 100 to one. Thirty-nine percent of the colleges in the sample had zero Republican faculty. Not a low number. Zero. The Heterodox Academy's analysis concluded that in disciplines such as sociology and anthropology, conservatives are either no longer attracted to academic careers or they are deterred from entering and discriminated against if found out.

Not a low number. Zero.

The ratio increased from roughly 4.5:1 in 1999 to 10:1 or higher by 2018 across most measures. A 2018 survey by

Samuel Abrams, a professor of politics at Sarah Lawrence College and senior fellow at the American Enterprise Institute, found that the liberal-to-conservative ratio among university administrators was 12:1. These are not polling anomalies or methodological artifacts. They are the consistent finding of multiple researchers using different methodologies across two decades.

Nothing about the intellectual quality distribution of the population explains these ratios. They are the outcome of decades of hiring practices that prioritized ideological alignment, implicitly or explicitly, over the kind of genuine intellectual diversity that would allow competing frameworks to challenge each other.

The consequence is not just that one political perspective dominates. The consequence is that the intellectual framework associated with that perspective has been allowed to harden into institutional orthodoxy without the challenge that competing frameworks would provide. Ideas that should have been tested and refined through argument have instead been insulated from argument by the simple mechanism of ensuring that the people who might argue differently are not in the room.

This is how the villainization of America became academic consensus rather than one school of thought among several. Not through the quality of its arguments but through the capture of the institutions that determine which arguments are taken seriously.

Chapter 8: The K-12 Pipeline

The university produced the framework. The K-12 system delivered it to children who were not yet old enough to evaluate it critically.

I want to be direct about that. Not to students. Not to adults who could push back. To children. The deliberate targeting of children who cannot yet question what they are being taught is the part of this operation that I find hardest to write about without losing my composure. The mechanism runs through three chokepoints: the state standards boards that determine what gets taught, the teacher certification programs that determine who teaches it, and the curriculum adoption committees that determine which materials are used. Capture those three chokepoints and you control what forty-nine million children learn about their country before they are old enough to ask whether the framework is true.

What the university capture in Chapter 7 produced, above all, was a teaching workforce. Universities produce everyone. But it mattered most because universities produce teachers. A teacher certified by an accredited education school has been processed through an institution where the framework documented in the previous chapter is not one perspective among several but the professional consensus. That consensus walks into classrooms across the country, every day, delivered by people who absorbed it so thoroughly that they do not experience it as ideology. They experience it as the correct way to teach.

The Standards Apparatus

In 2009, the Bill and Melinda Gates Foundation committed $200 million to the development of national educational standards. The resulting Common Core State Standards were adopted by forty-five states by 2012, not because state legislatures voted for them but because adoption was a condition for competing in the federal Race to the Top grant program. A billion dollars in federal incentives accomplished what a democratic vote might not have: the voluntary surrender of state curriculum authority to a nationally coordinated framework.

Mathematicians objected to the math standards. Reading specialists objected to the emphasis on informational text over literature. The standards were contested on pedagogical grounds. to the math standards. Reading specialists objected to the emphasis on informational text over literature. But the most consequential feature of Common Core was not its academic content. It was the infrastructure it built. A single national curriculum framework created a single pressure point for ideological influence that the previous state-by-state patchwork had not provided. Once a framework was embedded in Common Core-aligned materials, it reached classrooms in forty-five states at once.

The AP United States History framework redesign in 2014 showed what that pressure point could do. The College Board, a private nonprofit with no democratic accountability, revised the framework for the course taken by hundreds of thousands of college-bound high school students annually, reducing the emphasis on the chronological narrative of American political and military history in favor of thematic analysis organized around race, class, gender, and economics. Oklahoma's legislature voted to defund the course in the state.

Oklahoma's legislature and the Republican National Committee both condemned the framework. The College Board issued a revised version in 2015. The episode revealed the mechanism: a single curriculum body could reframe American history for the college-bound population in every AP-offering high school without any public vote, and could do so again after a political controversy by making adjustments subtle enough that the controversy subsided. The framework was not withdrawn. It was refined.

The Certification Pipeline

Every teacher certified in most states passes through the Council for the Accreditation of Educator Preparation. Without CAEP accreditation, an education school cannot certify teachers eligible for licensure in most states. CAEP incorporated equity-oriented pedagogical frameworks into its accreditation standards in the 2000s, requiring accredited programs to demonstrate commitment to what the standards called social justice pedagogy. A teacher education program that did not satisfy these requirements risked its accreditation. The mechanism is the same one documented in Chapter 12 for law schools: accreditation as a lever for ideological compliance, applied without legislative authorization.

The National Education Association and the American Federation of Teachers together represent approximately 4.6 million members. They are the largest professional union complex in the country, and among the most politically active. NEA political spending, reported in the organization's annual LM-2 disclosure forms filed with the Department of Labor and in Federal Election Commission records, runs between $50 and $60 million annually, directed at more than ninety-five percent to Democratic candidates and causes. Their collective bargaining agreements in major school districts include provisions that affect which materials teachers may use, what review rights parents have, and what consequences follow for teachers who deviate from approved approaches. They are not primarily academic organizations. They are political organizations with a teaching workforce attached, and the workforce they shape is the one that enters classrooms.

Teachers who come out of ideologically captured education schools do not deliver explicit political lectures.

It is that teachers arrive with a default framework: the curriculum is a site of political contestation, students need to develop critical consciousness about the systems that affect them, and the teacher's role is to help students question the assumptions they have absorbed from their families and communities. That default framework does not require a directive. It is the natural expression of the professional consensus the teacher absorbed.

The Curriculum as Delivery Mechanism

By 2020, three parallel mechanisms had embedded the framework into K-12 curricula across the country. The first was explicit legislative mandate. California's Ethnic Studies Model Curriculum, passed in 2021 and made a graduation requirement, came out of a committee that used academic critical theory as its explicit organizing framework. The curriculum drew extensively on concepts from ethnic studies scholarship developed in California's universities and directed students to interrogate systems of power, analyze positionality, and build community solidarity with others who share their experiences of marginalization. Illinois became the first state to mandate LGBTQ history education in 2019, followed by New Jersey in 2020 and four other states in subsequent years. These were not culture war provocations. They were legislative outcomes of decades of advocacy work by people who had absorbed the framework and wanted it delivered to students who had not yet encountered it.

Second was embedded teacher disposition. A teacher who has been trained to see the curriculum as politically contested will make a thousand small choices, which questions to ask, which perspectives to elevate, which historical figures to treat as heroes versus objects of critical analysis, that add up to a specific picture of what America is, delivered not as ideology but as education. This mechanism reaches schools where no explicit mandate exists.

The third mechanism was social-emotional learning. SEL frameworks, promoted by the Collaborative for Academic, Social, and Emotional Learning and adopted by school districts across the country as a response to documented student mental health concerns, inserted psychological frameworks into the school day under the heading of wellbeing. The specific psychological frameworks incorporated, identity development theory, trauma-informed pedagogy, restorative practices, created space for ideological content to arrive in the curriculum as therapeutic rather than political, and therefore outside the scope of normal parent review. The Ohio-based Positive Action SEL curriculum, adopted by hundreds of school districts, includes lessons directing students to identify 'systems of oppression' and 'internalized oppression' as part of its social awareness module, content that parents reviewing a curriculum described as social-emotional learning would not expect to find.

California's SEL Standards, approved by the state's board of education in 2023, include 'social change' and 'collective action' as core SEL competencies. A parent can object to a curriculum. Objecting to their child's emotional wellbeing is harder.

The child who entered a public school in 2020 encountered an institution that had been prepared, across three decades, to deliver a specific account of what the country is. Not all at once. Not through a single directive. Through the accumulated effect of standards, certification, curriculum materials, and teacher training that had all been shaped by the same framework. The preparation was thorough. The delivery was daily. The people who built this framework knew what they were doing. The rest of us are still figuring it out.

Chapter 9: The Media

I started with newspapers. That is how most people my age consumed news. You read the paper in the morning and you formed your picture of the world from what you found there. I watched that change. Not because print died, though it did, but because the people making editorial decisions changed, and the decisions they made changed with them. The shift was gradual enough that for a long time I could not have named what had changed. I just knew I was reading something different from what I had read before.

The internet accelerated everything. More sources, faster news, and an almost immediate sorting of those sources into camps with distinct assumptions about what America is and what it deserves. I watched that sorting happen and I watched myself participate in it. I read more widely than most people I know. I have also blocked channels and accounts that had crossed into something I could only describe as actively hostile to the country. Not critical. Not even harsh. Something different from that. A sustained effort to make the reader conclude that America is not worth defending. When I encounter that, I block it. Not because I cannot handle the argument. Because I have evaluated the argument and found it not to be an argument at all but a conclusion dressed up as one.

The cumulative weight of what I read on social media about America's founding, its history, its institutions, is what finally made me understand what this book is about. No single story. The aggregate. The relentlessness of it. The way the same basic message arrives in a hundred different forms until it starts to feel like something everyone knows. That feeling of obviousness is manufactured. And the media apparatus that manufactured it knows exactly what it is doing. This chapter documents it.

American newsrooms did not invent the villainization of America. They absorbed it from the academic framework that produced the people who run newsrooms, write op-eds, decide which stories get covered and which do not, and determine what the default assumptions of professional journalism are. That absorption happened gradually over several decades and it accelerated in the 2000s and 2010s as the economics of journalism changed in ways that rewarded ideological intensity over factual sobriety.

No major newspaper has a policy that says American history is primarily a story of oppression. What they have instead is a collection of editors and reporters who absorbed that framework in college, who hire people who share it, who apply it without examining it because it is the water they swim in. No major newspaper has a policy that says American history is primarily a story of oppression. What major newspapers have is a collection of editors and reporters who absorbed that framework in college and hired people who share it. They apply it without examining it because it is the water they swim in. The coverage reflects it without anyone consciously choosing that.

What Gets Covered and What Does Not

The most consequential form of media bias is not distortion of the facts in the stories that get covered. It is the decision about which stories get covered in the first place. The editorial judgment about what counts as news is where the framework does most of its work, and it does that work invisibly because nobody has to explain why a story was not assigned.

American military successes receive less coverage than American military failures. This is partly a legitimate journalistic judgment: failures are more newsworthy than successes in any domain. But the coverage gap between American failures and comparable failures by other countries, and between American successes and those same countries' successes, reflects something beyond the standard definition of newsworthiness. American failures confirm the villainization framework. Other countries' failures do not serve that framework. The coverage reflects the framework.

American economic achievements receive less coverage than American economic failures. Immigration success stories, the immigrant who arrived with nothing and built something real, receive less coverage than immigration failure stories. Communities that have maintained civic health and cultural continuity receive less coverage than communities in crisis. The man who built a business from nothing, who coached youth sports and served on the school board and kept his neighborhood together, is not a story. The man who fell through every gap in the system is.

Most individual journalists are making good-faith judgments every day. The criteria themselves have been shaped by the framework. The framework says American society is best understood through the lens of its failures. So the failures are more newsworthy than the achievements. So the coverage reflects a picture of America that is more negative than the reality.

The Newsroom Speech

There is a scene from the first episode of HBO's The Newsroom, which aired in 2012, that was celebrated at the time as one of the most honest moments in recent television. A news anchor, asked by a college student why America is the greatest country in the world, launches into a monologue cataloguing American decline: infant mortality rankings, literacy rates, incarceration numbers, the gap between what America claims to be and what the statistics say it is. The scene ends with him insisting that the first step to solving any problem is recognizing there is one. The audience in the scene cheers. Critics called it brave. The clip was shared millions of times as the kind of truth-telling that American media was too cowardly to do.

Watch it again now. It is not brave truth-telling. It is the villainization framework in its purest form, dressed up as the only intelligent position available to an honest person. The anchor does not say America has serious problems worth addressing. He says America is not the greatest country, and the clear implication is that anyone who believes it is must be deluded or dishonest. He does not compare America to authoritarian alternatives. He compares it to Norway. He does not acknowledge what produced the achievements he ignores. He selects statistics that serve the conclusion and presents them as a complete account.

The scene was celebrated because it told a specific professional class exactly what they already believed, in the language they found most persuasive, dressed up as the courage to say what nobody else would say. That is not journalism. That is not honesty. It is confirmation dressed as revelation. And its production, broadcast, and celebration as a cultural touchstone tells you something specific about what the media apparatus that produced it actually values.

What it does not value, apparently, is the question that was never asked in that scene: compared to what? Compared to what other country, in what other century, for what other population, has America done worse? The anchor never asks it because the answer would complicate the indictment. And complicating the indictment is not what the scene is for.

The Economics of Outrage

The digital media environment accelerated the dynamic that the academic framework had already established. Digital journalism is funded by attention. Attention is captured by outrage. Outrage is most reliably produced by content that confirms the audience's existing beliefs about who the bad actors are and what they are doing. The villainization framework, already dominant in the institutions that produce journalists, found in digital media an economic incentive structure that rewarded its most extreme expressions.

Outrage became a revenue strategy. Stories that frame American institutions as corrupt, American history as shameful, American power as predatory outperform everything else by every measurable digital metric. Stories that complicate that frame do not. The reporters who produce them are not being cynical. They are responding to feedback from the audience, which has been segmented by algorithm into groups that have been fed a consistent diet of confirming content until confirming content is what they seek and reward.

The foreign actors who want to amplify the villainization of America do not need to produce their own content when the domestic media apparatus is producing it for them at scale. What they can do, and what the Senate Intelligence Committee reports document them doing, is amplify the content that American media already produces. They reach audiences who would not otherwise encounter it. They strip the context that might complicate the frame. They connect it to the broader narrative of American evil that serves their strategic purposes.

What Honest Journalism Would Look Like

Honest journalism about America would look different from what currently dominates. It would cover American failures with the seriousness they deserve and American achievements with equal seriousness. It would apply the same critical framework to the villainization narrative that it applies to other narratives, asking who benefits, what evidence supports the claim, what evidence complicates it, and whether the conclusion follows from the facts. It would distinguish between structural problems and permanent features of American society, and it would cover the people and communities who are successfully addressing structural problems with the same energy it covers the people who are failing.

This kind of journalism exists. It is produced by reporters and editors who have resisted the framework and continue to apply the standards of evidence that journalism at its best has always required. It is not dominant. The economic incentives of digital media and the ideological homogeneity of the major institutions work against it. But it exists, and its existence is evidence that the problem is not journalism itself but the specific institutional and economic conditions that journalism currently operates in.

Whether that changes is an open question. The economic model that rewards outrage content is not weakening. The institutional pipeline that produces ideologically homogenous newsrooms is not changing. The honest journalism that exists is real, but it is swimming against the current. So far the current is winning.

A press that has decided what the story is before reporting it is not a free press. It is a propaganda apparatus that happens to employ people who believe they are journalists.

Chapter 10: The Culture Machine

The Media chapter documented how newsrooms absorbed the academic framework and delivered it as journalism. That is one vector. There is another, more pervasive, and historically more powerful: the stories a culture tells about itself through film, television, music, and shared entertainment. The villainization of America did not require a hostile press alone. It required a hostile culture industry. And for the past fifty years, the American culture industry has done work that the IRA and RT could not have matched with unlimited budgets.

What distinguishes entertainment from news is that entertainment reaches people who are not trying to form political opinions. News audiences are self-selected, people who tune in because they want information. Entertainment audiences are there for something else: pleasure, distraction, story. The ideological content arrives embedded in that something else, pre-loaded in the assumptions of the characters, the institutions that stories treat as corrupt, the values that narrative rewards or punishes. People who would never read a political essay about the moral bankruptcy of the military will watch a film in which the military's moral bankruptcy is simply the architecture of the story. They absorb the premise before they have the chance to evaluate it.

Vietnam as the Template

Vietnam set the template. In the decade that followed, Hollywood produced the most sustained ideological campaign against military service in the history of American cinema. Between 1978 and 1989, Hollywood produced the most sustained ideological campaign against military service in the history of American cinema. Coming Home (1978), Apocalypse Now (1979), Platoon (1986), Full Metal Jacket (1987), Born on the Fourth of July (1989). The films varied in quality but converged on a single conclusion: the American soldier is either a victim of a corrupt system or a participant in its crimes. The individual who chose to serve was either broken by what he was asked to do, or indifferent to the people he was doing it to. Neither version left room for the men my grandfather served with.

These films were celebrated by the critical apparatus as serious art. The Academy Award for Best Picture went to Platoon in 1987. The films that depicted American military service as honorable, The Green Berets (1968), Top Gun (1986), were dismissed as propaganda by the same apparatus. The asymmetry was not accidental. The critics who shaped the reception of these films had absorbed the same academic framework that shaped the newsrooms. The critical apparatus and the culture industry were staffed by the same graduate programs, and those graduate programs had been shaped by the institutional capture documented in Chapter 7.

Vietnam mattered less as history than as foundation. What it established was the default story about American military power. Every film that followed about American military engagement, from Black Hawk Down (2001) to American Sniper (2014) to the endless iterations of the ambiguous soldier wrestling with what he did, operates in the shadow of the framework Vietnam established: American military power is presumptively suspect, and the honorable soldier is the one who questions the mission. The framework arrived via entertainment and became, through decades of repetition, the assumption.

Who Makes the Stories

Walk into any major film or television production and you are working inside one of the most politically homogeneous professional environments in the country. Federal Election Commission donation records, analyzed by OpenSecrets and verified by multiple journalism outlets, document that contributions from entertainment industry employees run at Democratic-to-Republican ratios that exceed the faculty ratios documented in Chapter 7, consistently above 15:1 in FEC cycles from 2008 through 2024. The people who make American television and film are not a representative sample of America. They are a self-selected community, filtered through training programs and professional networks that share a specific political orientation, and their political views are more uniform than almost any other professional group in the country.

This matters because the stories they choose to tell, the characters they make sympathetic, the institutions they depict as corrupt, and the values they reward or punish in narrative are not politically neutral choices. A writers room that is ninety percent progressive will consistently produce content in which the assumptions of the progressive framework are built into the architecture of the story rather than examined. The villain is reliably the corporation, the general, the priest, the law enforcement officer. The hero is reliably the person who challenges those institutions. The pattern is not imposed from outside the industry. It emerges from a professional community that has absorbed a specific framework about what American society is and reproduces it in every story it tells.

The Pentagon has an entertainment liaison office, the Entertainment Media Office, that reviews scripts and approves or denies military cooperation (equipment, bases, technical advice) based on whether the production depicts the military accurately and in a manner that reflects well on it. The office has denied cooperation to films including Born on the Fourth of July, Forrest Gump, and The Hurt Locker. Productions that receive military cooperation, Top Gun, Act of Valor, 13 Hours, typically depict military service more favorably. The liaison office is not censorship. Studios can make any film they choose without military cooperation. But the films that receive cooperation get production value that films without it do not, which affects what audiences see and what the industry learns to produce.

The Internal Documents

Internal Disney materials that circulated publicly in 2022 gave the most specific documentation of how ideological commitments translate into production decisions. that circulated publicly in 2022. A diversity and inclusion presentation to Disney employees described company inclusion goals: at least fifty percent of regular and recurring characters to come from underrepresented groups, specific representation targets for LGBTQ characters, and frameworks for evaluating whether content met those goals before distribution. A Disney executive stated in a recorded meeting that she had committed to adding what she called queerness to children's programming wherever she could, and had been doing so with or without explicit direction from above.

Disney is not a uniquely ideological company. It is a documented example of what the broader culture industry had been doing less explicitly for decades: using the institutional machinery of entertainment to deliver a specific picture of what normal looks like, what values deserve reward, and what institutions deserve trust. The specific goals documented in the Disney materials, representation targets, identity-based storytelling frameworks, the explicit intention to influence children's understanding of sexuality and identity, had been operational throughout Hollywood without documentation for years before anyone wrote them down.

The Music Industry

The culture industry's reach extends beyond film and television. Popular music has delivered the same framework through a different channel for fifty years. From the anti-war folk tradition of the 1960s through the hip-hop political tradition of the 1990s through the current generation of pop and country artists who routinely treat American institutions as targets of irony or contempt, the music industry has been running a parallel operation to Hollywood.

Country music is the most instructive case, because it is the genre most closely associated with military families, working-class American identity, and traditional patriotism. That sector has faced sustained pressure from its own industry infrastructure, labels, streaming platforms, award committees, to align with the framework or accept diminished distribution. When the Dixie Chicks publicly criticized the Iraq War at a London concert in 2003, country radio stations pulled their music, protests were organized, and their career in the country genre effectively ended. The episode established an enforcement mechanism: express the wrong political views on the wrong subject and the industry withdraws its infrastructure. The same mechanism runs in reverse for artists who express traditional American identity themes in other genres, where the enforcement moves in the opposite ideological direction. The mechanism is the same. The framework controls who gets amplified.

The Gap the Audience Keeps Showing

The culture industry's grip on American stories has a persistent problem: the audience keeps telling it what it wants, and what the audience wants is not what the industry wants to make. American Sniper (2014) earned $547 million in North America, the highest-grossing film of the year and the highest-grossing war film in American history. The critical apparatus either ignored its success or treated the audience's enthusiasm as evidence of political pathology. Sound of Freedom (2023), a film about child trafficking that the major studios declined to distribute, was independently financed, acquired by a small distributor, and became a viral phenomenon that grossed

$250 million worldwide, more than Indiana Jones and the Dial of Destiny in the same summer.

Audiences keep telling the industry what they want. What they want is not what the industry wants to make. And that gap is not a gap between sophisticated taste and mass entertainment. It is a gap between the values of a specific professional community and the values of the country that community claims to represent. The audience has not become less sophisticated. It has been served, for fifty years, stories about itself that it does not recognize, and it has noticed. The audiences that showed up for American Sniper and Sound of Freedom were not looking for propaganda. They were looking for films that did not treat their values as the problem that the story has to solve.

The culture industry has not processed this gap as feedback. It has processed it as evidence that the audience is wrong. That response is consistent with a professional community that has absorbed the framework so completely that audience rejection confirms the framework rather than challenging it: if the audience likes it, it probably serves the wrong politics. If the audience rejects what the critical apparatus values, the audience has been corrupted by the framework the industry is trying to correct.

Fifty years of stories. The country has learned what it was taught. That is what stories do. The people who made those stories understood this. They were not making entertainment. They were making a culture.

I do not know how you undo fifty years of that. I am not sure anyone does. But I know you cannot undo it by pretending it did not happen.

Chapter 11: The Political Apparatus

I remember the first Obama election clearly, because that was when I noticed the shift was no longer creeping. It gushed in like a dam had burst. Before 2008 the villainization framework had been building for decades, slow enough that you could tell yourself it was fringe. After 2008 it was in the mainstream, in the language of political speeches and newsrooms and corporate communications. Each election since has made it worse. The dam did not get rebuilt. The water kept coming.

Political movements require a story about who the enemy is. It is a structural feature of democratic politics, not a cynical observation. To mobilize people to take collective action, you need to give them a clear account of what they are mobilizing against, who is responsible for the problems they want to solve, and why the stakes are high enough to justify the effort. The question is not whether political movements tell that story, but whether the story they tell is accurate.

Over the past several decades, the progressive political coalition adopted the villainization framework as its primary mobilization story. The enemy is not specific policies that have failed or specific actors who have behaved badly. The enemy is the American system itself: its founding, its institutions, its values, and the people who defend them. This story has proven extraordinarily effective at mobilization. It is less effective at governance, because a coalition organized around the premise that the system is irredeemably corrupt has difficulty explaining why participation in that system is worth the effort.

From Reform to Indictment

The American left has a genuine and honorable tradition of reform politics: the labor movement, the civil rights movement, the women's suffrage movement, the environmental movement. These movements identified specific injustices, organized to address them, and used the institutions of American democracy, including the courts, the legislature, and the capacity for mass public pressure, to produce changes that expanded the promise of the founding to groups that had been excluded from it. That tradition has not disappeared.

Barack Obama's 2020 address to progressive activists explicitly warned against the shift from reform to indictment politics, arguing that slogans and hashtag activism divorced from the work of building coalitions cannot produce the changes the work requires. Scholars like John McWhorter and academics across the political spectrum have made versions of this argument from within progressive and Black intellectual traditions. The reform tradition exists. The argument here is not that it has vanished but that it no longer dominates.

That tradition of reform politics is not the tradition that dominates the contemporary progressive coalition. The tradition that dominates is one in which the injustices identified are not specific failures of the system but fundamental features of it. The argument is not that American capitalism has produced specific exploitative arrangements that should be regulated. The argument is that capitalism is inherently exploitative. The argument is not that American democracy has failed specific groups in specific ways. The argument is that American democracy is a mechanism of racial oppression. The argument is not that specific American foreign policy decisions have been wrong. The argument is that American power is inherently imperial.

That shift from specific reform to totalized indictment changes the kind of politics a coalition can produce. Reform politics aims at specific, achievable changes to specific arrangements. It can succeed and then move on to the next problem. Indictment politics cannot succeed in the same way, because there is no specific change that addresses a totalized critique. The only sufficient response to the claim that the system itself is the problem is the replacement of the system. And since the replacement of the system is not achievable through normal democratic politics, indictment politics produces a permanent condition of mobilization against outcomes that can never be satisfactory.

Anti-Americanism as Coalition Strategy

The villainization of America has become a reliable mobilization tool for specific political actors who have discovered that the intensity of feeling it produces is effective for fundraising, voter turnout, and media coverage, regardless of whether it produces policy outcomes. Many of the people who use the framework believe what they say. The argument here is that the framework has been adopted partly because it works as coalition strategy, and that its adoption for strategic reasons has consequences for what the coalition can accomplish.

A coalition whose primary unifying narrative is that America is irredeemably evil cannot coherently defend American institutions, because defending American institutions is by definition a betrayal of the coalition's foundational premise. It cannot make the case for American power in the world, because American power is by definition the extension of the evil that the coalition exists to oppose. It cannot honestly reckon with the failures of the alternatives to American institutions, because acknowledging that the alternatives are worse complicates the indictment.

A movement organized this way gets very good at identifying and articulating American failures, and very bad at doing anything about them, because the framework it operates within forecloses the strategies that have historically produced reform. Reform requires believing the system is worth reforming. The villainization framework says it is not.

The Foreign Policy Consequences

Foreign policy is where anti-Americanism as political strategy does the most damage. A political movement organized around the premise of American evil cannot make a coherent argument for American leadership in the world. It cannot argue for the defense of American allies or for the use of American power in service of the values the founding articulated. Every assertion of American interest or American leadership can be countered, within the framework's own logic, with the observation that American power has historically served the interests of the powerful and harmed the powerless.

This is the argument that Russia and China have been making in international forums for decades. They do not need to invent it. American politicians, academics, and journalists make it for them. The foreign policy consequences of a country divided about whether its own power is legitimate are visible in specific episodes. In 2013, the Obama administration drew a red line on Syrian chemical weapons use, then declined to enforce it after domestic political pressure from factions who characterized any intervention as American imperialism. The decision divided his own administration and drew sustained criticism from foreign policy analysts across the political spectrum.

In 2011, the US-led NATO intervention in Libya was justified partly by appeals to the responsibility to protect doctrine, then abandoned before any governing structure could be established, producing a failed state that became a launching point for migration crises and a model for future Russian interventions. The failure in both cases was partly strategic. It was also a product of a political system where a significant faction had concluded that American power is primarily a force for harm. Allies in NATO, in

Asia, and across the Middle East saw both episodes. They drew their conclusions about the reliability of American commitment. They are still drawing them.

I have watched this coalition grow more confident and the country grow less capable of defending itself in the same years. I do not think that is a coincidence.

Chapter 12: The Legal Enforcement Apparatus

The preceding chapters document the institutions that produced the villainization framework and delivered it to the population. This chapter documents the institutions that enforce it.

You can disagree with a professor. You can turn off the television. You can pull your kids from a school. What this chapter documents is the point at which disagreement stops being an option, where the legal machinery gets involved and the cost of resistance becomes a career, a funding source, a federal investigation. That is a different kind of power. This chapter is about how it got built and how it operates.

Law Schools and the Pipeline

Law school faculties are more uniformly progressive than any other professional school, including education schools. A 2005 study by John McGinnis, Matthew Schwartz, and Benjamin Tisdell examined faculty political registrations at the top sixteen law schools and found Democratic faculty outnumbered Republican faculty by 8:1. More recent analyses suggest the ratio has increased since then. The specific numbers matter less than the implication. The professional class that interprets laws, argues cases, staffs regulatory agencies, and fills federal judgeships is produced by institutions with the same ideological profile as the humanities departments whose graduates run newsrooms and corporate HR departments.

Every major legal framework now shaping American institutional life started in a law school, not in a court or agency. Critical race theory, as a legal academic framework distinct from its K-12 curriculum applications, came out of work by Derrick Bell, Kimberlé Crenshaw, Mari Matsuda, and others at Harvard Law School in the 1970s and 1980s, and refined in law review articles before courts encountered it. Title IX enforcement doctrine was developed through legal academic argument before administrative agencies adopted it. Disparate impact theory, which holds that any statistical disparity in outcomes constitutes evidence of discrimination regardless of intent, was refined in legal scholarship before courts accepted it. Law schools are not downstream from the ideological operation. They are one of its primary production sites.

The ABA Accreditation Mechanism

The American Bar Association accredits law schools. Without ABA accreditation, a law school's graduates cannot sit for the bar exam in most states. In 2022, the ABA added Standard 206 to its accreditation requirements: accredited law schools must demonstrate by concrete action a commitment to diversity and inclusion in faculty hiring and student admissions, with the standard specifying that diversity efforts must show outcomes, not merely effort. An ABA consultant described the standard as requiring measurable results.

That sentence is the mechanism. Read it again.

A law school that produced faculty and student bodies reflecting the natural distribution of the population without evidence of active diversity programming would be at risk of losing the credential that allows it to operate. The mechanism is identical to the CAEP teacher certification framework documented in Chapter 8: accreditation as a lever for ideological compliance, applied without legislative authorization, through a private body that controls access to a legally required credential.

Disparate Impact and the Enforcement Machine

Disparate impact is the most consequential legal doctrine for enforcing the framework's institutional prescriptions. The Supreme Court endorsed the doctrine in Griggs v. Duke Power Co. in 1971. Under disparate impact, an employer who uses a selection criterion, a test score, a physical fitness standard, a credential requirement, that produces statistically different outcomes for different demographic groups can be found liable for discrimination, regardless of whether the employer intended to discriminate and regardless of whether the criterion is job-related.

The practical application of this doctrine has been extensive. Police departments have been forced to lower physical fitness requirements and modify written examinations after civil rights litigation documented differential pass rates, the NYPD entered a 2012 consent decree requiring revision of its sergeant and lieutenant promotional exams after Title VII litigation established disparate impact. Fire departments have had to revise promotional exams. The Ricci v. DeStefano case (2009) was the landmark: after New Haven administered promotional exams and then refused to certify the results because no Black candidates scored high enough to qualify, the white and Hispanic firefighters who had passed sued. The Supreme Court ruled 5-4 in their favor, holding that discarding test results solely because of racial composition violates Title VII. Dozens of similar challenges have been brought at fire departments across the country. The Armed Services Vocational Aptitude Battery, the primary military entrance exam, has been reviewed under disparate impact analysis and its subtests have been modified over decades in response to legal pressure and EEOC guidance.

No proof of discriminatory intent is required. The statistical disparity just has to exist, and a plaintiff has to file suit. The threat of litigation alone is sufficient to change institutional behavior, most institutions settle rather than litigate, and settlements become policy.

Cumulatively, disparate impact makes any empirical standard that produces differential outcomes legally risky.

An institution that wants to select the most qualified candidates by any objective measure must first ask whether that measure will produce differential results by demographic group, and if it might, must weigh the legal risk of using it against the cost of using a less accurate but legally safer substitute. The doctrine does not prohibit merit-based selection. It makes merit-based selection expensive. The institutions that can afford the legal defense continue using objective standards. The institutions that cannot, most public sector employers, most universities, learn to avoid them.

Title IX as a Template

Title IX of the Education Amendments of 1972 prohibits sex discrimination in federally funded educational programs. Its original application was to varsity athletics. Through forty years of administrative expansion and legal interpretation, it became the primary mechanism for transforming how universities handle sexual misconduct accusations, with due process protections significantly curtailed relative to ordinary legal proceedings. Universities adopted policies, single-investigator models, preponderance of evidence standards, limited cross-examination rights. Courts did not require those specific policies. The Department of Education's Office for Civil Rights issued guidance suggesting they were required, and universities complied rather than risk losing federal funding.

The Title IX enforcement model is instructive not for its specific application but for its structure: a federal funding condition, interpreted expansively by an administrative agency, enforced through the threat of funding withdrawal, producing institutional compliance without judicial process. The model has been replicated across the federal regulatory apparatus. Diversity requirements in federal contracting. Title VI enforcement in K-12 schools conditioned on federal education funding.

DEI requirements attached to NIH and NSF research grants. The pattern is the same in each case: the legal threat does not need to be fully exercised for it to produce the behavioral change the framework requires. Compliance culture does the work that litigation would otherwise require.

The Foundation for Individual Rights and Expression has documented what this culture produces at American universities: 114 instances of university employees sanctioned, investigated, or fired for speech protected under standard First Amendment analysis in 2023 alone. The legal system did not impose those outcomes in most cases. The institutions imposed them on themselves, preemptively, in response to the legal and reputational risk the framework created.

I want to be precise about what 114 means. These are people who said something true, or at least arguable, and lost their jobs for it. Some of them were reckless. Some of them were naive. But a significant portion of them were doing exactly what universities are supposed to exist for: saying something that the people around them did not want to hear. Every one of those cases sent a message to everyone who was not sanctioned. The enforcement apparatus is most powerful precisely when it does not have to be used. A university does not need to receive a federal funding threat. It needs only to believe one is possible. That belief is enough.

The academy produces the framework. The legal system makes it stick. The people who built this understood that ideas do not become power until someone can punish you for rejecting them.

Chapter 13: The Corporate and NGO Machine

Money follows narrative. The villainization of America is not free. The academic departments that produce the framework require funding. The nonprofit organizations that translate the framework into policy advocacy require funding. The media organizations that spread the framework require funding. The training programs that install the framework in corporations, schools, and government agencies require funding. The question of who provides that funding, and why, is a question that honest analysis of the villainization project cannot avoid.

The answer is complicated, because the funding comes from multiple sources with different motives. Some of it comes from genuinely well-intentioned philanthropists who believe the framework is correct and that funding its spread will produce social improvement. Some of it comes from foreign sources, documented in part and suspected in greater part, who recognize the framework as useful for American strategic decline. Some of it comes from institutional actors who have discovered that the framework is profitable. Corporations and government agencies pay substantial sums to have it installed in their workforces. The installation never reaches a point of completion that would reduce demand for more installation.

The DEI Industry and Its Incentives

By 2022, the DEI industry was a global market valued at $9.4 billion, according to Global Industry Analysts, with projections for continued growth. That number represents consulting contracts, training programs, corporate officers, nonprofit advocates, academic researchers, and the full apparatus of an industry built on the premise that American institutions require sustained intervention to address the systemic racism, sexism, and other forms of structural bias that the framework identifies as their defining features.

That number is not a rounding error. It is an industry.

The incentive structure of that industry is worth examining. An industry whose revenue depends on the existence of structural bias in institutions has no financial interest in the successful elimination of structural bias in institutions. A consulting firm that sells diversity training to corporations benefits from those corporations continuing to require diversity training. A nonprofit that advocates for anti-racist institutional redesign benefits from institutions continuing to be identified as racist in ways requiring redesign. The framework provides an infinite supply of problems, because it defines American institutions as inherently biased and any evidence of continuing inequality as confirmation of bias, regardless of whether the specific inequality in question has a specific cause that could be addressed directly.

Most people in the DEI industry believe in what they are doing. The structural incentive does not require individual cynicism. It requires only that people respond to the incentives their environment provides, which is what people do everywhere.

The Foundation Funding

The major American foundations, organizations like the Ford Foundation, the Rockefeller Foundation, the MacArthur Foundation, and dozens of others built on the accumulated wealth of American capitalism, have directed substantial portions of their grant-making toward organizations and projects that embody the villainization framework. The irony of this, large pools of wealth produced by the American capitalist system funding the systematic critique of that system, is not lost on observers across the political spectrum. The explanation for it is not complicated.

Foundation program officers are drawn from the same academic and nonprofit pipeline that produces the personnel of every other cultural institution. They absorbed the framework in graduate school. They evaluate grant applications through the lens of the framework. The organizations they fund are the organizations whose work confirms the framework. The cumulative effect of decades of foundation grant-making operating according to these criteria is a nonprofit sector thoroughly organized around the villainization framework, funded by the wealth that framework identifies as the primary source of American evil.

The foreign component of the funding question is harder to document in full than the domestic components, because foreign actors have learned to route their contributions through intermediaries that obscure the origin. What is documented is enough to establish that the pattern is real.

Since 2017, Department of Justice FARA enforcement has documented specific cases of foreign governments routing money through intermediaries to influence American political and media activity without disclosure. Between 1966 and 2015, the DOJ brought only seven criminal FARA cases in the entire half-century. Since 2017 it has brought several dozen, reflecting both increased foreign activity and increased enforcement attention. The 2016 DOJ Inspector General audit of FARA enforcement documented a 60 percent drop in registered foreign agents and a 73 percent drop in registered foreign principals since the mid-1990s, followed by the reversal of that pattern as enforcement ramped up.

One indictment illustrates the mechanism better than any other. In September 2024, the Department of Justice unsealed an indictment in the Southern District of New York charging two RT employees, Kostiantyn Kalashnikov and Elena Afanasyeva, with conspiracy to violate FARA and conspiracy to commit money laundering. According to the indictment, RT funneled approximately $9.7 million through shell companies in Turkey, the United Arab Emirates, and Mauritius to a Tennessee-based content creation company later identified as Tenet Media. Wire transfer notes described payments as purchases of iPhones and electronics.

The money funded nearly 2,000 videos published across YouTube, TikTok, Instagram, and X, accumulating more than 16 million views. The videos covered immigration, inflation, domestic division, and other topics the indictment described as directed to the publicly stated goals of the Government of Russia and RT: to amplify domestic divisions in the United States. The influencers who produced the videos say they were deceived about the source of funding. The DOJ did not allege wrongdoing by them. The operation ran undetected for approximately a year.

The Tenet Media indictment is notable not because it is the largest foreign influence operation documented but because it is the most detailed. The structure it reveals, shell companies, fictional personas, payments disguised as commercial transactions, content designed to amplify American divisions without disclosing its Russian origin, is the structure that intelligence analysts believe foreign actors use across a much larger range of information activities than any single indictment documents. The documented cases are the visible portion of a pattern whose full dimensions remain classified or unknown. What can be said with confidence is that the documented portion establishes that the pattern exists and that it targets the amplification of American domestic division.

The Self-Sustaining System

What makes the corporate and NGO apparatus most consequential is not any single element of it but the way the elements reinforce each other. The foundations fund the academic departments that train the graduates who enter the corporations that hire the consultants trained by the nonprofits funded by the foundations. The loop is not perfectly closed and there are actors at every point who resist it. But it is close enough to closed that it generates its own momentum.

Every node of this network rewards the same conclusion. The academic who produces the most thorough indictment of American institutions gets the grant. The nonprofit that articulates the sharpest critique of American power gets the foundation funding. The corporation that performs the most elaborate DEI commitment gets the positive press coverage. The politician who adopts the most complete version of the framework gets the small-dollar donations.

One documented chain illustrates the mechanism. Ibram X. Kendi's Center for Antiracist Research at Boston University raised approximately $43 million from donors in its first two years following the publication of his bestselling How to Be an Antiracist (2019), which argued that the only remedy for past discrimination is present discrimination in the opposite direction. The largest single gift was $10 million from Twitter founder Jack Dorsey. The Rockefeller Foundation contributed $1.5 million. The Ford Foundation provided smaller grants. The framework from the book was subsequently required reading in corporate DEI training programs at hundreds of major American companies, including several with federal contracts. The same corporate DEI programs generated consulting contracts for firms trained in the framework, who trained HR departments, who used the framework to evaluate employees, whose performance reviews affected promotion decisions.

Boston University administrators faced no institutional pressure to evaluate whether the Center's work was producing the outcomes it claimed. The foundation's investment decisions face no accountability to whether the theory they funded was accurate. The loop runs from academic production to foundation funding to corporate training to HR enforcement with no external accountability at any node.

ESG added a financial pressure that operated independently of ideology. BlackRock, the world's largest asset manager, implemented ESG proxy voting guidelines beginning around 2017 that tied shareholder votes on corporate governance to DEI performance metrics. A company whose board lacked demographic diversity, or whose workforce data showed insufficient representation in management, risked a negative ESG score that affected its access to capital from ESG-oriented investors. The mechanism did not require anyone at BlackRock to believe the villainization framework. It required only that DEI performance metrics be embedded in the financial incentive structure that governs corporate behavior. Corporate legal and HR departments responded to the financial incentive the way corporate departments always respond to financial incentives: they complied. The DEI consulting industry that sold the training programs needed to satisfy the metrics grew accordingly.

At its most influential nodes, the system that is supposed to produce citizens capable of self-governance is instead producing people whose primary skill is indicting the idea of self-governance. I find that extraordinary. Not in a good way.

Part Three: The External Accelerators

The foreign actors who recognized a weapon being built and decided to help.

Chapter 14: Russia

This is not the first time. The same pattern played out in World War One and World War Two, when enemy powers worked to corrupt American institutions and sow discord from inside. What is different now is the force amplifier. The news media was that amplifier then. Social media is a far more powerful version of the same weapon today. The enemy does not need to reach everyone. They need to find the fractures, pour content into them, and let the echo chambers and cognitive biases do the rest. Most people have never been taught to recognize those mechanisms in themselves. That is part of what this chapter is about.

The Soviet Union spent the Cold War trying to convince the world that America was evil. They did not succeed on their own. They had help. And the help came from us.

The tools were crude: state television broadcasts, printed propaganda, funded front organizations, and the occasional useful idiot in a Western academic or cultural institution willing to transmit the message for ideological reasons. The message was consistent: American capitalism exploits the poor, American democracy is a facade for corporate power, American military force is imperial violence, American culture is decadent and spiritually bankrupt.

It found an audience. The genuine failures of American policy in Vietnam, the genuine racial injustices of Jim Crow, the genuine economic inequalities of American capitalism gave the Soviet message a hook in reality that pure invention would not have had. What the Soviets were doing was not primarily manufacturing false claims. They were identifying true failures, amplifying them, stripping the context that would complicate the picture, and presenting the selected, amplified, decontextualized failures as the complete picture of what America is.

Soviet active measures against the United States ran from the late 1950s through the Soviet collapse in 1991 and was far more extensive than its most visible contemporary expressions. Operation INFEKTION, the KGB's 1980s campaign to spread the claim that the US government had created AIDS as a biological weapon, reached audiences in more than fifty countries and was believed by a documented percentage of the American public for years after its Soviet origin was exposed.

Documented Soviet financing flowed to the Council for a Democratic Germany, the National Committee for a SANE Nuclear Policy (SANE), and dozens of other American peace and disarmament organizations received documented Soviet financing or direction during the 1960s through 1980s, documented in the Mitrokhin Archive and corroborated by Venona intercept analysis. The Soviet-funded World Peace Council coordinated the nuclear freeze movement in Western Europe and the United States in the early 1980s. It channeled the genuine concern about nuclear weapons in directions that served Soviet strategic interests: opposing NATO's deployment of Pershing missiles while not opposing Soviet SS-20 deployments.

The Mitrokhin Archive and Venona intercept analysis document Soviet attempts to infiltrate and direct American civil rights organizations during the same period, not because Soviet operators cared about civil rights but because racial grievance was the most productive domestic fracture point available.

That sentence should be read slowly. The Soviet Union looked at the suffering of Black Americans, looked at the unfinished work of civil rights, looked at the genuine moral wound in the country's history, and calculated: useful. That is what a hostile foreign power does with your unhealed wounds. It does not try to heal them. It tries to keep them open.

This operation did not end with the Soviet Union. It did not even pause.

RT and the Information Operation

Russia Today, rebranded as RT in 2009, is a state-funded Russian media organization that produces content in English, Spanish, Arabic, French, and German. Its explicit stated purpose, as articulated by its founders and its government sponsors, is to present an alternative to Western media narratives. Its actual operational purpose, as documented by Western intelligence agencies and media researchers, is to amplify content that delegitimizes Western governments and institutions and to present Russian government positions as credible alternatives. RT registered as a foreign agent with the Department of Justice in 2017 under the Foreign Agents Registration Act.

RT's coverage of the United States is a case study in the selective amplification technique the Soviets pioneered. It covers American police violence comprehensively. It covers American poverty comprehensively. It covers American political dysfunction comprehensively. It covers American foreign policy failures comprehensively. All of these subjects are worth covering. All of them involve real events that real American journalists cover as well. What RT does that American journalists do not is present these failures as the defining and complete picture of American society, without the context of American achievements, American reforms, or the comparative perspective that would allow an audience to evaluate the severity of the failures against alternatives.

RT's actual broadcast audience in the United States is a matter of genuine dispute. RT claims, based on studies it commissioned, a US weekly viewership of 8 to 11 million. Leaked internal RT documents obtained by The Daily Beast in 2015 told a different story: RT's own internal reporting to the Kremlin showed the network did not appear in Nielsen's US ratings at all, which begin at 18 million households, and that its average daily US viewership was estimated at under 30,000. Whatever the true broadcast figure, it understates RT's actual reach. RT's YouTube channel had accumulated over seven billion views before Western platforms removed it following the 2022 invasion of Ukraine, making it one of the most-watched news channels on the platform. Its content circulates extensively on social media, often stripped of RT branding, among audiences who encounter it as simply another source of news about American failures.

Researchers measured the effect. A 2021 study published in the journal Security Studies, using a controlled experiment with a nationally representative sample, found that Americans who were exposed to RT content became ten to twenty percent more likely to support US withdrawal from its role as a cooperative global leader than those who did not watch RT. The researchers found that this effect held across measures, across party lines, and persisted even when subjects were informed that RT is financed by the Russian government. The audience does not need to know it is consuming Russian state media for the content to do its work. It needs only to absorb the picture the content presents.

The Internet Research Agency and Social Media

What the IRA did was a quantum leap in efficiency. Its operations, documented in the Senate Intelligence Committee's five-volume report published between 2019 and 2020, represent a quantum leap in the efficiency of the Soviet-era amplification technique. The IRA employed hundreds of people working in shifts around the clock, operating thousands of fake accounts across every major social media platform, producing content designed to amplify the divisions and grievances that the domestic villainization framework had already identified.

None of it was invented. The IRA found content that American users had already produced, content that expressed racial grievance, anti-military sentiment, contempt for American institutions, hostility to capitalism and American power, and amplified it to audiences who would not otherwise have encountered it. It created fake accounts presenting themselves as American voices expressing these views at higher volumes and with greater intensity than the actual American population held them. It coordinated messaging across fake accounts to produce the appearance of consensus where no consensus existed.

What it chose to amplify is documented in the Senate report. Anti-police content. Black Lives Matter content, alongside anti-Black Lives Matter content, because the IRA was not trying to advance any particular political cause but to maximize conflict between existing American communities. Anti-military content. Content associating the American flag and American symbols with racism and oppression. Content associating American Christianity with bigotry and intolerance. Content promoting the specific narrative of American founding-as-crime that the 1619 Project would later bring to mainstream prominence.

No new content needed to be created. The IRA took what American institutions had already produced and operating as an industrial-scale amplification machine, ensuring that the content reached audiences who needed to be radicalized further, that it was presented as coming from real American voices, and that it drowned out the content that complicated the picture.

Hundreds of people. Working shifts. Pretending to be American. Taking real American grievances and turning up the volume on the angriest, most divisive versions of them. This is what a hostile foreign government decided to spend its intelligence resources doing to the United States. And the Americans who built the content they were amplifying gave them everything they needed.

After 2016, the operation evolved. A September 2024 federal indictment documents what replaced the social media campaign. After RT America was dropped by American cable providers following the 2022 Ukraine invasion, RT employees developed a different approach: fund American influencers directly, through shell companies and fake investor identities, to produce content that served Russian strategic interests without disclosing the connection. Two RT employees, Kostiantyn Kalashnikov and Elena Afanasyeva, were charged with funneling $9.7 million to a Tennessee content company through shell entities in Turkey, the UAE, and Mauritius.

Wire transfers were disguised as iPhone purchases. The company produced nearly 2,000 videos for platforms including YouTube, TikTok, Instagram, and X. The videos accumulated more than 16 million views. Their subject matter: immigration, inflation, domestic division, and content the indictment described as directed to the publicly stated goals of Russia and RT, to amplify domestic divisions in the United States. The influencers involved, some with audiences in the millions, have said they were deceived about the source of the funding. The operation ran for approximately a year before the indictment.

The Strategic Logic

Russia's strategic interest in the villainization of America is not complicated. An America that doubts its own legitimacy cannot defend its allies. An America that is consumed by internal conflict about its own nature cannot project coherent power in defense of its interests. An America whose military cannot recruit because the culture has delegitimized military service cannot maintain the force structure required to deter Russian regional ambitions in Europe.

Russia does not need America to become Russia. It needs America to become less capable of opposing what Russia wants to do. An America paralyzed by internal division, unable to agree on its own history, unable to defend its own institutions against the charge that they are irredeemably corrupt, is exactly what Russia needs. The villainization of America, whether produced by Russian active measures or by American academic frameworks or by both working in inadvertent concert, produces exactly that paralysis.

Russia is not trying to win the argument about whether America is evil. It is trying to ensure that Americans cannot stop arguing about it long enough to notice what Russia is doing while they argue.

Chapter 15: China

China alarms me more than Russia does. The Soviet Union was a clear enemy. Every American knew it. China is not perceived that way, and that is precisely what makes it more dangerous. The subtlety is the weapon. Russia bludgeons. China moves quietly through institutions, through investment, through platforms, through academic relationships. Most Americans do not think of China as an adversary at all, which means the operations this chapter documents are running in a country that has not put its defenses up. The USSR was never that subtle. China has learned from every mistake the Soviets made.

China's approach to the villainization of America is more sophisticated than Russia's and more dangerous in the long term. Russia amplifies American self-criticism. China has built the platform.

TikTok is the most significant information environment that the Chinese government has built for American audiences, but it is not the only one. Confucius Institutes, funded by the Chinese government and operating inside American universities, have shaped the academic environment in which American students learn about China, ensuring that critical perspectives on Chinese governance are underrepresented and that Chinese government positions are treated as legitimate scholarly perspectives. The Department of Justice has documented Chinese government-linked influence in American political institutions through multiple channels. Congressional testimony and DOJ enforcement actions have identified cases of Chinese government-affiliated entities funding American political organizations and advocacy groups through intermediaries designed to obscure the origin. The Senate Intelligence Committee's 2019 report on foreign influence documented the broader Chinese government campaign to build relationships with American officials at the federal, state, and local level through financial relationships. The specific mechanisms are documented in congressional testimony and in DOJ enforcement actions brought under FARA since 2017.

Chinese money has entered American media companies and entertainment in documented ways that create financial incentives for American institutions to align with Chinese government preferences. AMC Theatres was acquired by Chinese conglomerate Dalian Wanda Group in 2012, making the largest US cinema chain a subsidiary of a company with documented ties to Chinese government interests. Legendary Entertainment, the production company responsible for the Pacific Rim franchise and Godzilla, was acquired by Wanda in 2016. Chinese investment in Hollywood between 2010 and 2019 exceeded $10 billion by multiple industry estimates. The financial relationship creates an incentive structure that affects content decisions even without explicit direction. A studio with Chinese financing and Chinese box office revenue will make different choices about how to portray China, its government, and American-Chinese competition than a studio with no such relationship.

All of these channels serve the same strategic function: reducing America's capacity to see China clearly, to evaluate China's behavior honestly, and to respond to Chinese actions with the clarity that effective strategic competition requires.

TikTok and the Deliberate Contrast

The documented difference between what TikTok serves to Chinese users through its Douyin platform and what it serves to American users through TikTok is the most visible evidence of Chinese strategic intent. Chinese youth on Douyin receive content promoting patriotism, scientific achievement, historical accomplishment, and national pride. American youth on TikTok receive content optimized for emotional engagement and social conflict, with heavy representation of content about racial grievance, gender conflict, institutional corruption, and the failures of American institutions.

This difference is not the product of different user preferences in the two markets, though user preferences differ and are reflected in content. It is the product of deliberate algorithmic choices that serve one government's strategic interests. The Chinese government monitors and shapes Douyin content to ensure it promotes the national story it wants Chinese youth to absorb. The same company's American platform shapes TikTok content in ways that promote the story that serves Chinese strategic interests in the American market.

Researchers at the Australian Strategic Policy Institute, the Network Contagion Research Institute, and other institutions have documented the content differential in detail. The documentation is specific enough to establish the pattern beyond reasonable doubt. What remains disputed is whether the differential is the product of explicit Chinese government direction or the emergent product of an engagement-optimization algorithm operating under Chinese law and within Chinese strategic expectations. The distinction matters less than the outcome, which is documented and consistent.

Confucius Institutes and Academic Influence

Confucius Institutes are Chinese government-funded educational programs operating inside American universities. At their peak, more than a hundred American universities hosted Confucius Institutes, which provided funding for Chinese language instruction, cultural programming, and academic exchange. The funding came with conditions, documented in the contracts between universities and Hanban, the Chinese government agency that administers the program, that gave the Chinese government influence over programming and created financial incentives for the host universities to avoid content the Chinese government found objectionable.

The American Association of University Professors recommended in 2014 that universities close their Confucius Institutes unless they could renegotiate the contracts to remove the conditions. Most universities did not. The FBI and the Senate Permanent Subcommittee on Investigations documented in 2019 the mechanisms by which Confucius Institutes influenced the academic environment. They suppressed discussion of topics the Chinese government found sensitive. They created financial relationships between American universities and the Chinese government that created incentives for institutional self-censorship.

What gets suppressed through Confucius Institute influence is predictable: the topics on which an accurate understanding of China would be most inconvenient for Chinese strategic interests: the treatment of Uyghurs in Xinjiang, the history of Tiananmen Square, the status of Taiwan, the mechanisms of Chinese political control. A generation of American students educated in an academic environment shaped partly by Chinese government funding has received a systematically incomplete picture of what China is and what the Chinese government does. That incompleteness serves China's strategic interests in the competition with the United States.

The Deliberate Asymmetry

The most important thing to understand about China's approach to the villainization of America is that it is deliberately asymmetric. China promotes traditional masculine virtues, patriotism, and national pride in its own population while funding and amplifying content that undermines those same values in the American population. China restricts the hours its youth spend on video games. Its platform in America delivers gaming and distraction content at maximum engagement. China promotes discipline and deferred gratification domestically. The platform it operates in America promotes individual grievance, institutional distrust, and outrage.

Chinese strategic planners have explicitly articulated the goal of building a population with the traits required for long-term national competition, including physical fitness, academic achievement, and civic commitment, while working to erode those same traits in the primary competitor population. The TikTok content differential is one expression of that strategy. The Confucius Institute academic influence is another. The targeted investment in American political and cultural institutions through financial channels that create incentives for American actors to align with Chinese preferences is a third.

China has learned from the Soviet experiment. The Soviets seeded an ideology and waited for it to take root. China is not waiting. China is actively managing the information environment in the United States in real time, using tools the Soviets did not have, at a scale the Soviets could not have achieved, with a precision the Soviets would have envied.

The country that controls what a population believes about itself controls the population. China understands this. The question is whether enough Americans understand it before the gap closes.

Chapter 16: The Convergence

In 2016, I watched the coverage of the presidential election in real time, switching between networks. What struck me was not the partisanship. I had watched partisan coverage for thirty years. What struck me, and what I could not fully name at the time, was the uniformity of the framework underneath the partisanship. Every outlet was operating from the same set of assumptions about what America was and what was wrong with it. They were arguing about who was responsible for the failures. Nobody was questioning whether the failures were the complete story. I remember thinking: when did this happen? When did the whole conversation shift to this ground and this ground only? I have spent the years since trying to answer that question. This chapter is part of the answer.

The villainization of America was not planned. No single meeting produced it. No single actor designed it. What produced it was the independent development of multiple forces, each pursuing its own objectives for its own reasons, that happened to converge on the same target and compound each other's effects in ways that none of them could have produced alone.

Genuine intellectuals working on real problems developed the academic framework. The media coverage patterns were shaped by professional journalists making individual editorial judgments. The political coalition strategies were developed by political actors trying to win elections. The foreign operations were designed by intelligence services pursuing their countries' strategic interests. None of these actors coordinated with the others in any organized way. All of them produced outputs that reinforced the outputs of the others.

This is what makes the convergence so difficult to counter. You cannot identify the architect and dismantle the plan because there is no single architect and no single plan. You can document the outputs and trace the incentive structures that produced them, and you can ask who benefits from the convergence and why, but you cannot produce the kind of clean causal account that would allow a simple policy intervention to reverse it. What you can do is name it clearly enough that the people it is targeting understand what is being done to them.

The Feedback Loops

Here is how the loop works. The academic framework produces graduates who enter journalism and produce coverage that reflects the framework. The coverage normalizes the framework for audiences who have not read the academic literature. The normalized framework makes the political coalition strategy of organizing around it more viable, because the audience for it has grown. The political coalition's adoption of the framework gives it institutional legitimacy that makes it easier for the foreign actors to amplify it without being dismissed as foreign propaganda.

The foreign amplification reaches audiences that the domestic content did not reach, including populations that are skeptical of the domestic sources but consume foreign-amplified content without recognizing its origin. The 2024 Tenet Media case documented in Chapter 9 illustrates the mechanism precisely: RT employees funneled nearly $10 million to a Tennessee content company that produced 2,000 videos amplifying American domestic divisions through well-known American influencers, none of whom knew the source of their funding. The influencers were not foreign agents.

They were American voices, with millions of American followers, producing content that American algorithms identified as engaging and distributed further. The foreign hand was invisible. The domestic distribution was entirely real. Those audiences, newly exposed to the villainization content, produced social media content of their own that the algorithm further distributed. The additional distribution reached the journalists who use social media to gauge what their audience cares about. That produced more coverage of the topics the narrative emphasizes. That fed back into the academic framework as evidence that the topics it identified are indeed the important ones.

A specific documented example of the loop closing: The IRA's Senate Intelligence Committee documentation shows that its accounts were most effective not when they created new content but when they amplified existing domestic content that was already performing well by engagement metrics. The domestic content was genuine American expression of genuine American grievance. The amplification made that genuine content reach audiences that would not otherwise have seen it, in volumes that made fringe positions appear mainstream. The appearance of mainstreaming changed the behavior of American journalists who track social media for story ideas, which produced news coverage, which gave the positions actual mainstream legitimacy, which completed the loop. No conspiracy. No coordination beyond the initial amplification decision. The architecture of the information environment did the rest.

Each loop tightens the others. The convergence produces not a static picture but an accelerating one, in which the villainization narrative becomes progressively more dominant in the institutional environments that shape how the next generation understands the country they are inheriting.

The Absence of a Counter-Narrative Infrastructure

Part of what makes the convergence so effective is the absence of a comparably organized counter-narrative infrastructure. The institutions that once provided an alternative to the villainization narrative, the civic organizations, the religious institutions, the local newspapers, the community institutions that transmitted the national story from one generation to the next, have been weakening for decades. The villainization framework has contributed to that weakening, because institutions that are systematically portrayed as corrupt and oppressive lose the social authority that makes them effective transmitters of any narrative.

The result is an asymmetry. The villainization narrative has strong institutional infrastructure: the major universities, the major media organizations, the major foundations, the major corporations, the major NGOs, and the foreign amplification machines. The alternative narrative has weaker institutional infrastructure: smaller media organizations, communities of faith of varying size and influence, military and veterans communities, and the informal transmission of values through families and local institutions that have not been fully captured by the framework.

The asymmetry is not permanent. Institutions are built and rebuilt. Alternative media has grown significantly. Communities of faith that have maintained their organizational integrity have also maintained their capacity to transmit values. Military and veterans communities have produced cultural content that reaches substantial audiences. The alternative infrastructure is real. It is outgunned by the convergence infrastructure. The question is whether it can grow fast enough to matter.

What Naming It Accomplishes

You cannot fight something you cannot see. The first step in countering the convergence is naming it clearly enough that people can recognize it when they encounter it. The villainization of America is not criticism of America. It is a specific operation with specific characteristics: the totalization of American failure, the denial of the possibility of improvement, the application of the framework without exception to any evidence that might complicate it, and the systematic removal of the context that would allow an honest evaluation of American failures against alternatives and against American achievements.

Once that pattern is named, it becomes visible. A student who has been taught to recognize the difference between reckoning and villainization can encounter the villainization framework in a classroom and evaluate it as the ideological operation it is rather than absorbing it as the objective truth it presents itself as. A news consumer who understands the pattern can recognize selective amplification when they encounter it. A citizen who understands the foreign dimension can recognize when content is serving foreign strategic interests regardless of who is nominally producing it.

Naming is not sufficient. It is necessary.

You cannot defend against an operation you cannot see. That is the first problem. The second is that the people running it are counting on you to keep arguing about whether it exists.

Part Four: The Cost

What the villainization of America has actually produced, in numbers.

Chapter 17: The Data

Arguments can be dismissed. Data is harder.

The operation is not theoretical. It has been running for decades and its outputs are measurable. What follows is a selection of the most relevant data, sourced from government databases, peer-reviewed research, and reputable survey organizations. The data does not prove that the villainization of America caused every negative trend documented here. Social causation is complex and multivariate. What the data does establish is that the trends are real, that they are moving in the direction the villainization project would predict, and that they are not accounted for by any explanation that does not include the systematic delegitimization of American institutions.

Look at the numbers. Then decide what you think produced them.

Civic Trust and Institutional Confidence

Gallup has tracked American confidence in major institutions since 1973. The trend lines are not ambiguous. Confidence in the Supreme Court fell from forty-four percent in 1973 to twenty-five percent in 2022, the lowest ever recorded. Confidence in Congress fell from forty-two percent in 1973 to eight percent in 2023. Confidence in the presidency fell from fifty-two percent in 1975 to twenty-three percent in 2022. Confidence in organized religion fell from sixty-five percent in 1973 to thirty-two percent in 2023. Confidence in the public schools fell from fifty-eight percent in 1973 to twenty-six percent in 2022. Confidence in newspapers fell from thirty-nine percent in 1990 to eighteen percent in 2023. Confidence in television news fell from forty-six percent in 1993 to fourteen percent in 2023.

The declines are not uniform across institutions and not uniform across time. Some institutions have maintained higher confidence than others. But the aggregate picture is unmistakable: Americans have lost faith in the institutions that organize their collective life at a rate and to a degree that has no precedent in the survey data. The timing of the declines tracks the penetration of the villainization framework into the institutions most responsible for shaping public understanding of American life: the schools, the media, the universities.

A serious reader will raise the obvious alternative explanations, and they deserve a direct answer. The intelligence failure that produced the Iraq War, publicly documented by 2004, gave Americans a specific documented reason to distrust the government and the media that had amplified its claims. The 2008 financial crisis, in which major financial institutions were bailed out by taxpayer money after engaging in practices that regulators had permitted and rating agencies had certified, gave Americans a specific documented reason to distrust financial and regulatory institutions. The COVID pandemic produced documented failures of public health communication, including reversals on masking guidance and vaccine efficacy claims, that gave Americans specific documented reasons to distrust public health institutions. These failures were real and the distrust they produced was earned.

This book does not claim the villainization framework is the only explanation for declining institutional confidence. It claims the framework is a significant and underexamined contributor that compounds the effects of genuine institutional failure. The distinction matters because genuine failures can be addressed through institutional reform. The framework prevents reform by insisting that the failures are not failures of specific institutions but features of what American institutions are. A country that processes genuine institutional failure this way will not reform its institutions. It will delegitimize them. The data shows both processes running at once.

Social trust, the measure of how much Americans trust their fellow citizens in general, has followed a similar trajectory. The percentage of Americans who say that most people can be trusted fell from forty-six percent in 1972 to thirty-one percent in 2023. The percentage who say you can't be too careful in dealing with people rose correspondingly. This is the civic foundation eroding. A democracy requires that citizens trust each other enough to submit to common rules, accept electoral outcomes, and engage in the good-faith disagreement that self-governance requires. The erosion of social trust is the erosion of the capacity for self-governance itself.

That is not a metaphor. It is arithmetic.

Think about what that actually means. A population that does not trust institutions can still organize around a candidate. It can still flood the streets for a cause. What it cannot do, reliably, is the slower, less dramatic work of building the shared infrastructure that collective life requires. Zoning boards. School boards. Water districts. The machinery of self-governance that operates below the level of spectacle.

National Pride and Civic Identity

Gallup has also tracked American pride in national identity. In 2001, fifty-five percent of Americans said they were extremely proud to be American. By 2023 that number had fallen to thirty-nine percent, the lowest ever recorded. Among Americans under thirty, it is lower still. Among college-educated Americans under thirty, it is lower than that.

The college education variable is telling. The population that has been most thoroughly processed through the institutions most thoroughly captured by the villainization framework shows the sharpest decline in national pride. The distribution is not random. It is the measurable output of a specific educational experience. Graduates of institutions that have adopted the framework are more likely to have absorbed the conclusion the framework is designed to produce: that America is not worth being proud of.

Pew Research Center surveys on national identity show similar patterns. The percentage of Americans who say being American is very important to their identity has been declining, most sharply among young adults. The percentage who say the American way of life needs to be protected from foreign influence has also declined. The percentage who describe themselves as patriotic has declined. The percentage who say they would be willing to fight for their country in a war has declined. These are the measurable outputs of a population being told that what it is part of is not worth defending.

Military Recruitment and Civic Participation

The connection between the cultural trends and the military recruitment crisis is direct and documented. The Pentagon's Joint Advertising, Market Research and Studies office, which conducts annual surveys of youth attitudes toward military service, found that propensity to serve among young Americans aged sixteen to twenty-one declined from a high of sixteen percent in November 2003 to nine percent in the spring of 2022. The Army's own research attributes part of this decline to cultural factors: eligible young people do not want to serve in an institution that the culture around them has characterized as morally compromised.

Voting rates among young Americans have fluctuated but show a long-term pattern of disengagement interrupted by periods of intense mobilization around specific issues. The pattern is consistent with a population that has been taught that the system is corrupt and that engagement with the system is either futile or complicit, interspersed with periods when a specific grievance is intense enough to overcome that baseline disengagement.

Community organization membership, volunteer rates, and civic group participation have been declining for decades, a trend documented by Robert Putnam in Bowling Alone in 2000 and confirmed by subsequent research. The specific mechanisms vary but the aggregate picture is consistent with a population less embedded in the civic infrastructure that produces community loyalty, shared obligation, and the sense of belonging to something larger than individual interest.

The Psychological Cost

The data on institutional trust, national pride, and military recruitment documents the civic damage. There is a parallel set of numbers that documents the psychological damage, what happens inside people when the framework succeeds. The story being tested here is not just whether Americans trust their institutions. It is whether the systematic replacement of a national story that provides meaning with a national story that provides indictment has produced measurable human suffering. It has.

The Centers for Disease Control's Youth Risk Behavior Survey documents youth mental health trends across the country. Between 2011 and 2021, the percentage of high school students who reported persistent feelings of sadness or hopelessness increased from 28 percent to 44 percent, a 57 percent increase in a decade. The percentage who seriously considered suicide increased from 16 percent to 22 percent. These are not marginal changes. They represent a structural shift in the psychological condition of American adolescents that has no precedent in the survey's history.

Jonathan Haidt, a social psychologist at NYU's Stern School of Business, and Jean Twenge, a psychologist at San Diego State University, have independently documented the relationship between social media adoption and adolescent mental health collapse. Haidt's research, synthesized in The Anxious Generation (2024), argues that the smartphone-mediated social environment that replaced direct social interaction for American adolescents beginning around 2012 produced the mental health crisis visible in the CDC data. Twenge's longitudinal research documents the same inflection point across multiple measures. Their work is contested in the academic literature on specifics but the basic finding, that something changed for American adolescents around 2012, and that the change tracks the mass adoption of social media, is not seriously disputed.

What the Haidt-Twenge research does not fully account for is the specific content that social media delivered to those adolescents. The algorithmic amplification documented in the Russia and China chapters applies to the mental health crisis as directly as it applies to political polarization. The IRA's content strategy prioritized the amplification of content that produced emotional distress. The Chinese TikTok algorithm serves American youth content optimized for engagement, which means content that produces strong emotional responses, and the content that produces the strongest emotional responses among adolescents is content about social anxiety, body image, political grievance, and existential despair. The mental health crisis and the information environment crisis are not parallel problems. They are the same problem.

The loneliness epidemic compounds both. The Surgeon General of the United States issued an advisory in 2023 declaring loneliness and social isolation a public health crisis, citing data showing that roughly half of American adults reported measurable levels of loneliness even before the COVID pandemic accelerated the trend. The Survey Center on American Life documented in 2021 that the percentage of Americans who said they had no close friends had increased fivefold since 1990, from 3 percent to 15 percent. Men were disproportionately affected: 15 percent of men reported having no close friends, compared to 10 percent of women. The institutions that historically produced and sustained friendship, religious communities, civic organizations, the military, the trades, are the institutions that the villainization framework has most systematically delegitimized.

The data on deaths of despair, deaths from suicide, drug overdose, and alcohol, rounds out the picture. Princeton economists Anne Case and Angus Deaton documented in their research beginning in 2015 that mortality rates had been rising, not falling, among middle-aged white Americans without college degrees, reversing a century of declining mortality rates for that demographic. The increase was concentrated in deaths of despair.

These are men who are dying younger than their fathers did. That is the sentence that should stop you.

The population experiencing the highest rates of deaths of despair, working-class men without college degrees in economically distressed communities, is exactly the population the villainization framework most thoroughly excludes from its preferred categories of concern. They are neither the oppressors nor the oppressed as the framework defines those categories. They are the men that a culture that has been taught to regard them as the problem cannot reach with the story that their lives are worth living.

What the Numbers Add Up To

Read these data points together and they describe not a collection of separate problems but a single system-level failure expressing itself through multiple indicators. A population that does not trust its institutions. That is not proud of its country. That does not want to defend it. That is not embedded in the civic organizations that produce shared obligation and community loyalty. That has been processed through educational institutions that have systematically undermined the story that makes collective action possible.

Taken together, this is not the profile of a population capable of sustained collective action. It is a population that has been prepared for something closer to managed decline: a collection of people and identity groups moving through an institutional landscape they do not believe in toward ends that do not extend beyond their own group's interests.

This is exactly the population that foreign adversaries identified as the strategic goal of the villainization operation. They looked at the country my grandfather fought for and they decided to empty it out from the inside. And the data shows they are succeeding.

The numbers are not a judgment on the people who produced them. They are a measure of what a well-executed operation can produce over sixty years. The people in the data did not choose this. It was done to them, slowly enough that most of them never noticed it happening.

Interlude: Eight People

The preceding chapter is numbers. This is what the numbers look like when they have faces.

What follows is drawn from documented public cases, court records, published journalism, and on-the-record interviews. Two profiles, James Whitfield and Rachel Torres, are drawn directly from named people who have spoken publicly on record. The remaining profiles are composites built from documented patterns, combining characteristics and experiences representative of populations whose situations the data in the previous chapter describes. None of the experiences depicted are fabricated. They are here because the argument of this book is about what happens to specific human beings when a country loses the capacity to tell an honest story about itself, and data without people is just arithmetic.

Five of these accounts are Americans who lost something to the villainization of America. Three are people who found something in resisting it.

Kevin Nguyen, Age 34. Software Engineer. San Jose, California.

Kevin Nguyen's parents arrived in the United States from Vietnam in 1979, two adults and a child, with a hundred and forty dollars and the belief that the country they had reached would give them something their country of birth no longer could. His father worked factory shifts while learning English at night. His mother cleaned offices. Kevin attended public schools, got a scholarship to UC Davis, and became a software engineer. By the time he was thirty he had a job, a mortgage, and a family.

He describes the experience of watching the country his parents chose become the country his colleagues had been taught to despise. The mandatory DEI training at his company that characterized the American system as structurally racist in terms that left no room for his family's experience of it. The social media environment that classified his political views as complicit in oppression because they did not match the framework his colleagues had absorbed in college. The slow, steady pressure to perform a story about America that his parents' lives contradicted.

He is not bitter. He is confused in a way that confusion does not quite capture. His parents chose America. The institutions that are supposed to represent America are telling him his parents chose wrong, or were deceived, or that the thing they chose was not what they thought it was. He does not know how to hold his parents' experience and the framework's account of America in the same frame. He has stopped trying. He says he is now a conservative mostly because the people who despise the country his parents sacrificed to reach are in the other party.

Master Sergeant Thomas Reeves, Ret. Age 52. Three Combat Tours. Fayetteville, North Carolina.

Thomas Reeves enlisted at eighteen and spent twenty-four years in the Army, including deployments to Iraq in 2003, Afghanistan in 2008 and 2012. He was good at his job. He won't say so directly but his record does. He retired as a Master Sergeant and moved home to North Carolina, where he works as a contractor and coaches high school football.

He describes what it felt like to watch the institutions that his son was passing through teach his son a story about what Thomas had done for twenty-four years. The curriculum that framed American military history as primarily imperial violence. The social media content his son consumed that characterized soldiers as either victims or war criminals. The college he attended where a professor described American military power in terms that

Reeves found not just wrong but obscene given what he had seen his friends die for.

His son graduated and went into finance. He does not want to serve. Thomas says he understands, that he would not push a son toward something he didn't believe in. What he can't get past is that the thing his son doesn't believe in is the thing Thomas gave twenty-four years to, and nobody who shaped his son's view of it ever asked Thomas what it was actually like, what the men he served with were actually like, or what they thought they were actually doing.

He says the hardest part is not the criticism. He can take criticism. The hardest part is being invisible. Being talked about by people who would rather not talk to him.

Sister Margaret O'Brien, Age 68. Catholic Sister. Chicago, Illinois.

Sister Margaret O'Brien has been running a food pantry on the south side of Chicago for thirty-one years. The pantry serves several hundred families a week. It is staffed primarily by volunteers from the parish and funded primarily by donations from Catholic institutions. It has never received a government grant that required it to change how it operates or who it serves.

She describes the progressive displacement of religious institutions from the civic infrastructure of the communities she serves. The government programs that require participation in bureaucratic processes that the families she serves cannot manage. The nonprofit organizations that have received foundation funding to address the same problems she addresses but that apply criteria and frameworks that exclude the people most in need of what she provides. The steady pressure, from funders and advocates and progressive politicians, to frame her work in ideological terms that she finds at odds with why she does it.

The specific pressure she describes is documentation. Newer programs funded by major foundations require beneficiaries to be categorized by demographics, to sign consent forms written in language the pantry's clients cannot read, to participate in outcome-tracking systems that treat them as data points in a research project rather than people in need of food. Sister O'Brien does not have the staff or resources to implement these systems. The foundation programs she is not eligible for funded organizations that do implement them, producing, in her assessment, less actual food delivered to fewer actual people but more data delivered to more actual foundations. She is not angry. She is tired in the way that people who have been doing something real for a long time get tired. She is also not stopping.

James Whitfield, Age 44. High School Principal.
Colleyville, Texas.

James Whitfield is Black. He became the principal of Colleyville Heritage High School in Texas in 2020, the first Black principal in the school's history. Later that year, the school district became the center of a national debate about critical race theory when a parent filed a complaint alleging that Whitfield had promoted the framework in his school. The school board voted not to renew his contract.

Whitfield has said publicly that he did not teach critical race theory, that he taught his students to be honest about history, and that there is a difference between honest history and ideological advocacy. He also said that the politicization of the debate, from both sides, made it impossible to have the conversation about history education that schools need to have.

His case is documented here not as evidence for either side of the curriculum debate but as evidence of what the debate costs people who are caught in the middle of it. A Black principal who wanted to teach honest history, working in a community that had been primed by the national argument to see honest history as ideological advocacy, lost his job. The framework produced the polarization that made his situation impossible. Neither the people who wanted him gone nor the people who wanted him vindicated asked him what he was actually trying to do.

Elena Rojas, Age 29. Teacher. Phoenix, Arizona.

Elena Rojas teaches fifth grade in a Phoenix public school. She is the daughter of Mexican immigrants. She received her teaching credential from Arizona State University, where the education school curriculum was organized around the critical pedagogy framework derived from Paulo Freire. She absorbed the framework and went into her classroom believing she was implementing the correct approach to teaching children who looked like her.

After three years she began to have doubts. The framework told her that her job was to help her students recognize their oppression and develop critical consciousness. Her students, the children of working-class immigrant families, wanted to learn to read and do math and understand science well enough to pass tests and get into good schools and build the lives their parents had come to America to give them. The framework she had been trained in did not have a good account of how critical consciousness helped with that.

She is still teaching. She has modified her practice substantially. She describes herself as someone who learned the framework, believed it, tried to apply it, discovered that it did not serve her students, and had to figure out how to teach well despite the training she received. She is not alone. She says the teachers who are doing the most good in her school are the ones who have set aside the framework, informally and without announcing it, and focused on whether their students can read.

Sergeant First Class Maria Chen, Age 38. Army Recruiter. Houston, Texas.

Maria Chen is one of nine thousand Army recruiters working to close the gap between the Army's personnel requirements and the population of young Americans willing and able to meet them. She has been a recruiter for four years, following eight years in logistics. She describes the recruiting environment as unlike anything the Army has encountered before, and not primarily for the reasons that get discussed in congressional testimony.

The physical disqualification rate, the percentage of potential recruits who cannot meet basic fitness and health standards, is a real problem and she spends time on it. The competition from the private sector labor market is a real problem and she spends time on that too. What she spends the most time on, in conversations she has not had in official settings, is the cultural problem. The young men who could qualify, who would have qualified in a different generation, who are physically capable and legally eligible and intellectually suited for military service, who simply do not believe that what the Army is and what it does is something they want to be part of.

She describes conversations with nineteen-year-olds who have spent their formative years consuming content that characterizes the American military as an institution of racial violence and imperial exploitation. Who cannot name a reason to serve that they have not been trained to dismiss as propaganda. Who have no veterans in their families or communities to give them an alternative picture. She is trying to recruit from a population that has been systematically prepared not to be recruited, and she is doing it with a pitch that the cultural environment has spent years delegitimizing. She says she still loves the job. She says it is harder every year.

William Park, Age 72. Korean Immigrant. Los Angeles, California.

William Park arrived in the United States from South Korea in 1978. He worked in a grocery store, saved money, opened his own store, built a small chain, sold it, and retired. He has four children, all of whom attended American universities, all of whom are professionals. He is a citizen. He votes in every election.

He describes watching his grandchildren, American-born, educated in American schools and universities, absorb a story about the country he chose that he does not recognize. They tell him about systemic racism and imperial violence and the corrupt founding. He tells them about what South Korea looked like in 1978 and what he found when he got here and they listen politely and then continue believing what their schools taught them. He is not angry. He says he understands that young people believe what the institutions that formed them tell them. He believed what his institutions told him too.

The specific thing he describes, and the reason his case belongs here, is a conversation with his granddaughter at Thanksgiving two years ago. She is twenty-three, a recent college graduate, employed at a nonprofit that works on housing equity. She told him, carefully and not unkindly, that his success story was real but that it could not be generalized, that the system that allowed him to build something was also the system that excluded others, and that pride in individual achievement distracted from the structural analysis required to address systemic inequality. He listened. He said: I came from a country with a different system. That system produced different outcomes. The comparison is the analysis. She did not have a response to that. The conversation moved to other things.

What he cannot reconcile is the gap between the story being told about America and the country he arrived in and spent his life in and chose for his children. He says: I came here with nothing. I built something. My children have opportunities my parents never dreamed of. This country made that possible. If that is not worth something, if that story is the story of oppression and exploitation, then I have misunderstood my own life. He does not think he has misunderstood his life. He thinks someone is telling his grandchildren a story that is designed to make them unable to see what he sees.

He is right about that. He is right and I am furious that he has to be right. A man who built something real with his hands in a real country is spending the end of his life watching his grandchildren being taught that what he built was a lie. That is what this operation produces. That is the cost. This book is, in part, an attempt to show them what he sees.

Staff Sergeant Rachel Torres, Ret. Age 41. Veteran. San Antonio, Texas.

Rachel Torres served eight years in the Army, including a deployment to Afghanistan in 2010. She came home with a Purple Heart and a traumatic brain injury that took three years to recover from. She is now a veterans' advocate who works with female veterans dealing with the VA system.

She describes the experience of being a veteran in the current cultural environment as one of constant translation. The culture has two stories about veterans: the broken victim who needs saving and the potential threat whose aggression needs managing. She does not recognize either story as the veterans she knows. The veterans she knows are people who made a choice, paid a price for it, and came home carrying that price and trying to build something with it. Some of them are struggling. Most of them are not. None of them are what the cultural framework says they are.

She says the hardest thing about the current moment is watching young people who would have made excellent soldiers choose not to serve because the culture has convinced them that the institution they would be joining is something to be ashamed of. She does not expect everyone to serve. She does not think everyone should. She expects that the people who could serve and would serve in a different cultural environment are being lost to a narrative that is not true, and that the country is paying a cost for that loss that it will not fully understand until the next time it needs more soldiers than it can find.

Eight people. Five who lost something to the villainization of America and three who are resisting it. All of them are real. All of them are in the data this book has built its argument on. None of them chose the forces that shaped their situation.

The villainization of America is not an abstract debate about history curricula and media bias. It is what happens to specific people when a country loses the capacity to tell an honest story about itself. These are some of those people. There are millions more.

I went into this chapter without strong expectations, and what I found was more uncomfortable than I expected. Yes, Russia. Yes, China. Yes, the political left. But the honest answer is that all political parties have bought into some version of these arguments, or into counter-arguments just as toxic. When I see a policy proposal that would decommission nuclear power plants, for example, I think about who benefits from that long-term. A nation without reliable energy production is a nation that can be crippled without firing a shot. That is almost certainly Russian influence, whether the people pushing the policy know it or not. The benefit is the tell. Most of the people who benefit have no idea they are serving someone else's strategic interests. That is what makes the operation work.

Every analyst looking at a complex social phenomenon eventually asks the same question. Not who caused it, because causation in social systems is rarely clean enough to assign to a single actor. Who benefits. Follow the benefit and you find the architecture of the incentive structure that sustains the phenomenon regardless of how it originated.

The villainization of America benefits multiple parties with different interests, different mechanisms, and different levels of awareness that they are operating in concert. The parties are worth naming separately, because conflating them produces a conspiracy theory where the actual situation is something more diffuse and more dangerous: a convergence of interests that sustains a harmful outcome without requiring coordination.

Russia and China: The Strategic Beneficiaries

The primary foreign beneficiaries of the villainization of America are Russia and China, for reasons documented in Chapters 14 and 15. The villainization reduces America's capacity to project power in support of its interests and its allies. It reduces the military's ability to recruit the people required to maintain force structure. It reduces the civic cohesion required for the sustained collective action that strategic competition demands. It produces a political environment in which a significant fraction of the American political system opposes the assertion of American power in the world on the grounds that American power is inherently harmful.

Russia derives a more immediate benefit: the paralysis of American willingness to support the alliance structures that constrain Russian behavior in Europe. An America divided about whether its power is legitimate is an America that will hesitate at every decision point about whether to commit resources, reputation, and risk in defense of allies who depend on American commitment. Russia's regional ambitions in Europe depend on that hesitation. The villainization of America is, in this direct sense, a security subsidy for Russian regional aggression.

China derives a longer-term benefit: the gradual erosion of American competitive capacity across the full range of domains in which the two countries are in strategic competition. Education, military recruitment, technological innovation, civic cohesion, institutional effectiveness, and the soft power that comes from being a country that other countries want to emulate. The villainization of America attacks all of these domains by producing a population less invested in the collective project and less confident in the shared story that motivates collective effort.

The Institutional Beneficiaries

The domestic institutional beneficiaries of the villainization of America are the organizations whose existence and revenue depend on the persistence of the problems the framework identifies. The DEI consulting industry. The foundations and nonprofits organized around the premise of American institutional racism. The academic departments whose research programs depend on the inexhaustibility of the structural critique. The media organizations whose revenue model depends on the engagement that American institutional failure reliably produces.

None of these institutional actors benefits from the resolution of the problems they identify. A DEI consulting firm that successfully eliminated structural bias in its client institutions would eliminate its own market. An academic department that produced a research program demonstrating that the structural critique had overstated the degree of institutional racism would undermine its own funding base. A media organization whose coverage produced a population more confident in American institutions would lose the engagement that institutional distrust reliably generates.

The argument here requires a qualification. Some of what the DEI apparatus produced was real. Workplace discrimination against women and minorities was a documented problem in 1970. It is a smaller problem in 2026, partly because of the legal and cultural pressure that came from exactly the kind of institutional advocacy the book has been criticizing. The argument in Chapter 4, that the DEI apparatus serves its own perpetuation, is broadly true as an institutional dynamic. It does not mean every specific intervention was useless. The honest version of this argument holds both things: the interventions that worked and the institutional incentive structure that now works against acknowledging when they have worked.

Most of them believe what they say. The structural incentive does not need cynicism. It needs people who respond to the incentives their environment provides, which is what people do.

The Political Beneficiaries

The political beneficiaries of the villainization of America are the actors who have discovered that organizing a coalition around the premise of American evil is more effective for raising money, generating media coverage, and producing voter turnout than organizing a coalition around the premise of American improvement.

The difference between these two coalition strategies is the difference between reform politics and indictment politics. Reform politics says: these specific things are wrong and here is how we will fix them. Indictment politics says: the system is corrupt and the people who built it and defend it are your enemies. Reform politics can succeed and then face the difficult problem of what to do next. Indictment politics cannot succeed in the same way, because there is always more to indict, which means the mobilization energy is permanent.

Permanent mobilization energy is extremely valuable in democratic politics. The political actors who have access to it have a structural advantage in fundraising, turnout, and media attention over political actors who are trying to make the more complicated argument that American institutions, despite their failures, are worth improving rather than replacing. The villainization framework is partly a political strategy. The people who deploy it benefit from its deployment regardless of whether it produces the social outcomes they claim to be seeking.

The Reparations Framework as a Case Study

The reparations debate illustrates this structure with unusual clarity. Nikole Hannah-Jones, whose 1619 Project sits at the center of the villainization framework's academic form, has said publicly that her ultimate goal for the project was passage of reparations legislation. The curriculum and the policy demand are explicitly linked by their own architect.

This book takes no position on whether reparations are just or unjust as a policy. What it observes is the incentive structure of the demand. A political movement organized around a demand for reparations for the descendants of enslaved African Americans has an obvious interest in the reparations demand remaining politically alive rather than being resolved. Resolution would end the mobilization. Permanent grievance sustains it. The political actors who benefit from the framework benefit more from the demand staying alive than from any specific policy outcome. That is why the policy has remained a demand for thirty years without becoming a proposal with a specific mechanism, a specific amount, a specific recipient class, or a specific source of payment.

The selective scope of the demand is also worth examining honestly. Slavery is not an American institution or a European one. It is among the oldest and most universal practices in human history, practiced by every major civilization across every continent. If the framework were about slavery as a universal historical harm requiring remedy, the catalogue of demands would extend in every direction.

Between 1500 and 1800, an estimated one to 1.25 million Europeans were captured and sold into actual chattel slavery by North African Barbary corsairs. This is not disputed by mainstream historians, the figure comes from Robert Davis of Ohio State University, whose book Christian Slaves, Muslim Masters documents the trade in detail. These were not indentured servants with fixed terms. They were chattel slaves, sold at auction, forced into labor for life, captured from coastal villages across Italy, Spain, Portugal, France, England, and Ireland. In 1631, corsairs raided the village of Baltimore on the Irish coast and carried off the entire population. Long stretches of the Italian and Spanish coastline were abandoned by their inhabitants at the height of the raids. Thomas Jefferson created the United States Navy to end the Barbary threat, and tribute payments to the Barbary States represented twenty percent of US government revenues in 1800.

No country has established a reparations framework for the descendants of the 1.25 million Europeans enslaved by North African corsairs. No university issues land acknowledgments for the abandoned coastal villages of Italy. No curriculum has been built around the 1631 sack of Baltimore. The absence of these demands is not because the historical harm was less real. It is because the reparations framework is not organized around slavery as a universal historical harm. It is organized around a specific political project in American domestic politics, with specific beneficiaries who have specific interests in its continuation.

The honest version of the argument against American slavery's legacy does not require the selective framework. The actual history is damning enough, the ongoing measurable effects are real, and the policy question of how to address them is legitimate and worth having. What the selective framework adds to that honest argument is not clarity. It adds the political utility of a demand that cannot be resolved, which benefits the political actors who deploy it far more than it benefits the descendants of enslaved people they claim to represent.

Who Pays

Every system of beneficiaries has its mirror. Someone always pays.

The Americans who pay are the people whose civic institutions are being delegitimized, whose national story is being replaced with one that leaves them no reason to invest in the collective project, whose children are being educated in a framework that systematically undermines the values and skills required for effective citizenship. The veteran who comes home to a culture that does not know what to make of him. The immigrant who chose America and watches the country she chose being characterized as not worth choosing. The young person who wants to serve and has been taught that service is complicity.

The country pays. A nation with declining institutional confidence, declining social trust, declining civic participation, declining military recruitment, and declining national pride is a nation with reduced capacity to address its problems, defend its interests, and maintain the civic engagement that self-governance requires. The reduction is not catastrophic yet. It is steady, cumulative, and accelerating.

America's adversaries pay nothing. They receive a strategic benefit, delivered at low cost, produced primarily by American institutions, funded primarily by American wealth, sustained primarily by Americans who believe they are making their country better.

The most successful attack on a country is the one the country conducts on itself. The target does not need to know who built it.

Part Five: The Couter-Narrative

What the alternative looks like. It exists. It matters.

Chapter 19: Nations That Held

I want to be honest about something before this chapter makes its argument. I think the examples here are only partially correct. Germany, which this book holds up as a model of honest reckoning, is failing badly by other measures: terrible demographics, far-right parties rising, an economy that bought its stability with tax rates most Americans would not tolerate. Most of the European nations that are presented as success stories paid for that success in ways that would not translate here. I am not arguing against the reckoning lesson. I am noting that every example is complicated, and a reader who goes and checks will find the complications. The chapter's argument is about one specific thing these nations did right. It is not a claim that they got everything right.

Nothing about this is inevitable. Other democracies have confronted comparable failures, engaged honestly with difficult history, and maintained the civic bonds that allow collective action while doing so. The examples are worth examining because they demonstrate that the alternative is not naivete about national failure. It is something more sophisticated: the capacity to hold failure and achievement in the same frame without collapsing into either triumphalism or despair.

Israel: Democratic Self-Criticism Without Self-Destruction

Israel is a small democracy surrounded by enemies committed to its destruction, with a history that includes genuine crimes against the Palestinian population alongside genuine achievements in science, technology, agriculture, and democratic governance. Israeli public discourse is among the most vigorous in the world. Israeli newspapers, academics, artists, and politicians criticize Israeli policy, Israeli military conduct, and Israeli political culture with a frankness that would be unremarkable in any healthy democracy.

What Israeli public discourse does not typically produce is the conclusion that Israel itself is not worth defending. The criticism operates within a framework in which the existence and security of the state is not a question. Whatever criticisms are being made, whatever failures are being identified and debated, the underlying premise that the project is worth continuing is not the subject of the debate. Criticism and defense of the national project coexist because the civic culture maintains the distinction between criticizing specific policies and indicting the entire enterprise.

Israel has been able to maintain this distinction partly because the external threat is obvious and immediate: there are parties who openly advocate for the elimination of the Israeli state, and that fact makes the distinction between reform and abolition visceral rather than abstract. But Israel's civic culture also transmits the national story actively and continuously, through education, through military service that creates shared experience across social lines, through cultural institutions that maintain the connection between the present population and the historical experience that produced the state. The story is not uncritical. It is coherent.

Poland: National Identity Under Pressure

Poland spent the second half of the twentieth century under Soviet occupation, with its national story systematically replaced by the story the occupying power wanted Poles to believe about themselves and their history. When the occupation ended in 1989, Poles did not emerge from it having absorbed the replacement story.

They emerged having preserved the original story, transmitted through underground education, through the Catholic Church, through family, and through cultural institutions that the occupation could not fully capture.

The preservation of Polish national identity under conditions of active suppression is a case study in what civic culture can do when its institutions are committed to it. The Poles who maintained the story did not do so by refusing to acknowledge Polish failures, including the complicated relationship of some Poles to the fate of Jews during the Second World War. They maintained it by insisting that the failures were part of a complicated history that included achievements and that did not justify the conclusion that the Polish national project was not worth continuing.

Poland's current political environment is complicated and contested and not a model to be adopted wholesale. What the Polish experience demonstrates is that national stories can survive active suppression when civic institutions are committed to transmitting them. The question for America is whether its civic institutions, captured to varying degrees by the villainization framework, are still committed to transmitting the alternative.

Japan: Achievement and Accountability Together

Japan confronted, in the decades following the Second World War, the necessity of reckoning with what it had done in Asia between 1931 and 1945. The reckoning was imperfect and remains contested. Japanese textbooks have historically underrepresented the full scope of Japanese wartime atrocities. Japanese political culture has been resistant to the kind of full accounting that Germany has undertaken. These are legitimate criticisms that historians across the political spectrum have made.

What Japan also did, in the same postwar decades, was rebuild a devastated economy into the world's second-largest, develop extraordinary cultural achievements in technology, design, and popular culture that spread Japanese soft power globally, and maintain a stable democratic governance structure that has managed multiple severe crises without the civic breakdown that simpler predictions would have anticipated. The reckoning with failure and the achievement of a new story coexisted, imperfectly but functionally.

The mechanism that allowed this coexistence is worth examining. Japanese civic culture transmits national identity not through denial of wartime conduct but through parallel institutions that carry different parts of the national story. The education system teaches national history including its failures.

Workplace culture transmits collective obligation and group identity that extends beyond individual grievance. Annual ceremonies at Hiroshima and Nagasaki frame Japan as a nation that suffered the consequences of war and rebuilt, producing a national identity organized around resilience and reconstruction rather than permanent guilt. The imperial institution, reformed but maintained, provides continuity with a history that predates the wartime period and gives Japanese citizens a story longer than their worst chapter. None of these mechanisms are perfect. None of them require the erasure of what Japan did. They provide a framework in which the crimes are part of the record and not the complete account of what Japan is.

The Japanese experience suggests that a nation can carry the weight of genuine historical crimes without being defined by them, that the crimes can be acknowledged without becoming the complete account of what the nation is, and that the achievement of something new does not require the erasure of what was done wrong. It requires, instead, the kind of civic culture that can hold complexity without collapsing into a single totalizing judgment.

Germany: The Standard for Reckoning

Germany is the case the introduction to this book invoked as the model for genuine national reckoning. It deserves examination in detail, because it is the strongest example available of a country that confronted the worst thing it had ever done, built institutional mechanisms for honest accounting, and maintained a functioning democracy and civic culture capable of collective action on the other side of that accounting.

The German approach to its Nazi past was not immediate or complete. The early postwar Federal Republic prosecuted fewer war criminals than subsequent historians thought necessary, and West German society engaged in substantial collective silence about the specific experiences of the 1933-1945 period through the 1950s. What changed the trajectory was a generational confrontation that began in the 1960s, accelerated with the Auschwitz trials of 1963-1965, and produced by the 1970s and 1980s a set of institutional mechanisms with no direct parallel elsewhere.

Germany made Holocaust denial a criminal offense, Volksverhetzung, incitement to hatred, carrying sentences of up to five years. The charge applies to anyone who publicly denies, trivializes, or approves of the extermination of Jews. This is not a symbolic law. The German courts enforce it. The law draws a specific line: honest engagement with what happened, including skeptical or critical engagement, is protected. Denial that it happened is criminal. The distinction is exactly the reckoning/villainization boundary applied in law: you can criticize Germany's past in any terms you choose. You cannot erase it.

German schools teach the Holocaust from elementary through secondary education, with required visits to concentration camp memorial sites built into the curriculum in most states. The Berlin Holocaust Memorial, the Memorial to the Murdered Jews of Europe, occupies 4.7 acres at the center of the German capital, adjacent to the Brandenburg Gate. The Topography of Terror documentation center occupies the site of the former Gestapo and SS headquarters. The stumbling stones, Stolpersteine, are small brass plaques embedded in sidewalks throughout Germany and across twenty-six countries, each one bearing the name of a victim of Nazi persecution and their fate. More than 100,000 stumbling stones have been placed since the project began in 1992. They are not in museums. They are in the pavement outside the buildings where people lived before they were taken.

Germany also maintains the capacity to act as a country. It has not dissolved into permanent guilt that forecloses participation in collective endeavor. German citizens vote, pay taxes, serve in the Bundeswehr, celebrate German cultural achievements in music, engineering, and literature, and take genuine pride in what Germany has built since 1945 without needing to pretend 1933-1945 did not happen. The phrase never again is not rhetorical in Germany. It is policy. Germany has been one of the largest per-capita donors to Israel's security and has maintained that commitment through multiple Israeli governments whose policies German politicians found objectionable. The reckoning did not produce passivity. It produced a specific obligation that German civic culture has maintained across generations.

The German case is instructive for the American debate precisely because Germany had more to reckon with than the United States does. Germany's crimes were not the product of a founding generation's contradictions or the legacy of practices that the country's founding ideals eventually made untenable. They were the deliberate policy of a democratic government, executed within the living memory of people still alive. If Germany could build a civic culture capable of honest accounting and continued collective action, the argument that America cannot hold its failures and its achievements in the same frame, that the weight of slavery and its legacy makes any national story worth telling impossible, has no foundation in comparative experience. Germany did it. It is harder than what America is being asked to do. They did it anyway.

What These Examples Share

What Israel, Poland, Japan, and Germany share, despite their very different histories and political structures, is the maintenance of a civic culture that transmits a coherent national story across generations. The story is not uncritical. All four countries have strong traditions of internal criticism that identify failures, argue about history, and produce genuine disagreement about how the national story should be understood. What the criticism operates within is a framework that does not put the continuation of the national project itself in question.

America has that framework. It is called the founding ideals. The claim that all men are created equal and endowed with inalienable rights, that government derives its just powers from the consent of the governed, that the purpose of the political order is to secure the conditions under which human beings can pursue their own conception of a good life. These ideals are aspirational rather than descriptive. The country has consistently failed to live up to them fully. The failures are worth naming and addressing. What the failures do not establish is that the ideals themselves are fraudulent, that the political order built on them is not worth improving, or that the project is not worth continuing.

Denying American failure is not the alternative to the villainization of America. The alternative is the insistence that failure is not the complete story. Germany proved it. Japan proved it. The question is whether America is willing to do the same work.

Chapter 20: The Larger Catastrophe: What the Selective Framework Conceals

I have been fascinated by the Columbian Exchange since I first read about it years ago, and what draws me to it is that it is true in a way that makes the simplified story look small. What happened when Europe and the Americas collided was not a unique crime. It was a compressed version of something that has happened throughout human history wherever isolated populations meet. When the land bridge existed between Asia and North America, the same dynamics played out. Humans migrated and raised all kinds of hell. Continental drift has been causing these collisions for hundreds of millions of years. What made the post-1492 exchange different was not its nature but its speed, driven by ships and navigation and the fastest communication and transportation the world had yet seen. The catastrophe was real. The framework that treats it as uniquely European evil is not honest history. It is a selective reading of a universal human pattern.

The villainization of America presents the history of European contact with the indigenous peoples of North America as a moral event without parallel, a crime so foundational that it defines the country, requires permanent civic acknowledgment, and justifies a wholesale reexamination of whether American institutions deserve continuation. The history it draws on is real. The framing requires a specific and rarely examined assumption: that what happened in North America is the defining case of its kind. It is not. There is a larger catastrophe. It was driven primarily by Spain and Portugal. It was three times worse than the Black Death. And the countries most responsible for it are not the ones who face the villainization framework.

The full event is three times larger than the portion the framework selects. Reckoning with all of it is not an argument for minimizing the history of English colonial settlement. It is the precondition for honest accounting. And honest accounting produces a different set of questions than the framework asks.

The Great Dying

When Christopher Columbus landed on Hispaniola in 1492, approximately 60 million people lived across North, Central, and South America. For comparison, the entire population of Europe at the same moment was between 70 and 88 million people. The Americas were comparable in population to Europe, sustained by civilizations that ranged from the organized agriculture of the Mississippi Valley to the architectural and astronomical achievements of the Maya to the Inca Empire, which governed roughly 12 million people across 2,500 miles of Andean terrain through a system of roads, relay stations, and administrative records that stands as one of the great organizational achievements of the pre-modern world.

By 1600, one century after Columbus, approximately 56 million of those 60 million people were dead. That is a mortality rate of 90 percent. The University College London study that produced the best data-driven estimate of this figure, published in Quaternary Science Reviews by researchers Koch, Brierley, Maslin, and Lewis, called the Great Dying the largest human mortality event in proportion to global population in all of recorded history, second only to World War II in absolute numbers. It represented the death of approximately 10 percent of the entire human population of the planet.

Compare it to the Black Death. The bubonic plague that swept Europe in the mid-14th century killed between 25 and 50 million people, roughly 30 percent of Europe's population. It reshaped European civilization, depopulated entire regions, and altered the trajectory of European history for two centuries. It is remembered as the worst catastrophe in European history and taught that

166

way everywhere. The Great Dying killed 90 percent of the Americas' population, three times the proportional death rate of the Black Death, and it receives a fraction of the moral vocabulary, a fraction of the historical attention, and none of the permanent civic penance framework that the villainization narrative applies to the English colonial history that followed it by more than a century.

The scale was so catastrophic it altered the Earth's climate. When 56 million people die and no one is left to farm the land, the land reverts. Approximately 56 million hectares of previously cultivated land, an area roughly the size of modern France, were abandoned across the Americas within a century of contact. The reforestation of that land pulled enough carbon dioxide from the atmosphere to contribute to the coldest period of the Little Ice Age. The UCL researchers documented this: the death of a continent's population cooled the planet.

Who Was Responsible

English colonial settlement was not the primary cause. English permanent settlement of North America did not begin until 1607 at Jamestown and 1620 at Plymouth, more than a century after the catastrophe was already underway. By the time the Pilgrims landed on the Massachusetts coast, much of the coastal New England population had already been devastated by the epidemic of 1616 to 1619, which killed an estimated 90 percent of the people in many coastal communities. The Wampanoag federation survived, and Massasoit negotiated with the colonists from a position that was already weakened by the epidemic. The Pilgrims did not settle an empty wilderness. They settled a coastline that disease had already transformed.

The primary drivers of the Great Dying were Spain and Portugal. Hernán Cortés arrived on the Gulf Coast of Mexico in 1519 with roughly 500 soldiers and within two years had destroyed an empire of approximately 25 million people. Smallpox arrived with the conquistadors in 1520 and within seven years killed between a quarter and a half of the Aztec population. Francisco Pizarro arrived in Peru in 1532 with roughly 180 men and destroyed the Inca Empire. The speed of the destruction in both cases was possible because disease had already preceded the armies, traveling through indigenous trade networks faster than European soldiers could march.

In the Caribbean, historian Andrés Reséndez of the University of California, Davis, has documented that between 1492 and 1550 the conditions of Spanish forced labor, mining, overwork, famine, and direct violence, operated alongside disease in ways that prevented any recovery. European populations had rebounded from the Black Death over a generation because they were not also subjected to mass enslavement. Caribbean populations were. Reséndez argues that it was the combination of epidemic disease and forced labor that produced such rapid and complete demographic collapse, not disease alone. The Spanish were aware of smallpox by 1519; the recorded killing before that date was done primarily by people, not pathogens. The English colonial settlement of North America, which drives the villainization framework's primary narrative, was a secondary wave of a catastrophe that had already been running for 130 years.

The Countries That Did It Are Not the Ones Indicted

Mexico is the direct successor state of the Spanish conquest of the Aztec Empire. The government of Mexico sits in Mexico City, built on the ruins of Tenochtitlan. Mexico's national identity incorporates Aztec heritage, the eagle and serpent of the Aztec founding myth appear on the Mexican flag. The country celebrates its indigenous history as a source of national pride while being the political and cultural successor to the civilization that destroyed it. Brazil is the direct successor state of the Portuguese colonization that drove the destruction of hundreds of indigenous peoples across South America. Argentina, Peru, and Chile are the successor states of Spanish colonial rule. None of these countries face a villainization framework comparable to the one applied to the United States. None of them conduct civic rituals of collective guilt for the founding violence that produced their nations.

The United States, whose English colonial history was a secondary event that began more than a century after the primary catastrophe, whose founding documents articulated principles that became the basis for the expansion of rights to previously excluded groups, faces a framework of permanent moral indictment that the countries primarily responsible for the Great Dying do not face. The selectivity is not explained by the historical record. It is explained by the political purposes the framework serves.

What South America Actually Did

Two South American countries are worth examining because they demonstrate what genuine engagement with indigenous history can produce when it is organized around building rather than indicting.

Bolivia's constitution of 2009, approved by national referendum with 61 percent of the vote, is among the most comprehensive indigenous rights frameworks ever enacted at a national level. It recognized 36 indigenous nations by name, granted collective land rights that cannot be alienated or subdivided, established indigenous jurisdiction as legally parallel to ordinary courts, and enshrined Buen Vivir, Living Well, drawn from Andean indigenous philosophy, as a principle guiding state action. Bolivia elected Evo Morales, its first indigenous president, in 2005. He governed for thirteen years. The constitutional recognition of indigenous peoples was not symbolic. It was a structural reorganization of the relationship between the state and the peoples the Spanish conquest had displaced.

Ecuador's constitution of 2008, approved with 64 percent of the vote, gave nature itself constitutional rights, the first national document in history to do so. Articles 71 through 74 recognized the inalienable rights of ecosystems to exist and regenerate, drawing directly from the Quechua concept of Pachamama and the indigenous principle of sumak kawsay. These are not the outcomes of a villainization framework. They are the outcomes of a recognition framework, a decision to integrate indigenous peoples and indigenous knowledge into national identity rather than hold them permanently as historical victims whose suffering justifies political mobilization.

Compare that to what thirty years of the US villainization framework has produced. The framework has produced academic departments, curriculum changes, land acknowledgment statements, and reparations proposals that have not advanced to legislation. It has not produced a single piece of federal legislation equivalent to Bolivia's collective land rights provisions. It has not produced a constitutional amendment. It has not produced a structural change in the legal relationship between the federal government and indigenous peoples comparable to what Bolivia enacted by popular referendum in 2009.

The Gap Between Rhetoric and Reality

The deepest indictment of the villainization framework is what is happening to indigenous peoples right now, in the countries that conducted the larger historical crime, while the framework devotes its energy to the smaller one.

Brazil's 1988 constitution explicitly protects indigenous land rights. Brazil adopted the UN Declaration on the Rights of Indigenous Peoples in 2007. On paper, Brazil's framework for indigenous rights is progressive. In practice: deforestation inside officially designated indigenous territories increased 129 percent between 2013 and 2021. The Pastoral Land Commission documented more than 300 killings related to land conflicts in the Amazon since 2009. Of those 300 killings, 14 went to trial. Armed militias working for agribusiness and mining interests invade indigenous territories and are rarely prosecuted. The Guaraní people of Brazil, who have lost nearly their entire traditional territory to cattle ranches and sugar cane plantations, have a suicide rate 19 times the Brazilian national average.

This ongoing, present-tense dispossession of living people, in the country primarily responsible for the Great Dying, generates a fraction of the moral energy and none of the cultural framework of permanent guilt that the US villainization narrative devotes to events from 150 years ago in the country responsible for a fraction of the original catastrophe. The gap is not explained by the severity of the harm. It is explained by the political purposes the framework serves.

What Honest Reckoning Produces

Bolivia and Ecuador are not paradise. Bolivia's constitutional framework has been contested at every stage of implementation. Ecuador's rights of nature provisions have been inconsistently enforced. The gap between constitutional principle and daily reality in both countries is documented and real. What both countries produced that the villainization framework has not produced is a direction. A constitutional integration of indigenous peoples into national identity that defines them as foundational to what the country is rather than as permanent victims whose suffering defines what the country was.

The framework the villainization operation offers points in one direction: permanent indictment, permanent mobilization, permanent guilt as the organizing principle of national identity. It offers the boarding school system and the treaty violations as the permanent definition of what America is, rather than as failures of a country that also produced the Declaration of Independence, the abolition movement, the civil rights movement, and the constitutional framework that made all three possible. It offers grievance without resolution, because resolution would end the mobilization, and ending the mobilization would deprive the framework's architects of the tool they spent decades building.

Here is the strongest counter-argument: the United States is the world's current dominant power, and that ongoing power creates ongoing responsibility that historical actors like Spain and Portugal no longer exercise at the same scale. This is a real argument and it deserves a direct answer. Brazil is the eighth-largest economy in the world and the dominant power in South America. Mexico is the fifteenth-largest economy and a member of G20. Spain and Portugal are full members of NATO and the European Union. Argentina, Peru, and Chile are middle-income democracies with functioning governments. None of them is a failed state incapable of accounting for its history. More directly: the present-tense dispossession of indigenous peoples documented in this chapter is happening in Brazil, now, with the Brazilian government's knowledge, under Brazilian law that purports to protect the people being dispossessed.

The gap between protective law and brutal practice is not a historical artifact. It is current Brazilian policy failure. The ongoing-power argument does not explain why Brazil's ongoing failure against the peoples most directly harmed by the larger catastrophe generates so much less moral energy than the United States' historical failure against populations that are not today being killed in land conflicts. The selectivity is not explained by where power currently resides. It is explained by where the political mobilization energy is most useful.

Comparing English North America to Spanish South America exonerates neither. It establishes that the scale of historical wrong is not what drives the intensity of the framework. Spain and Portugal were responsible for a mortality event three times worse than the Black Death. The US villainization framework was not built around them. It concentrated around the United States because the United States was where the domestic frameworks found their most receptive institutional environment, where the foreign amplifiers found the most useful opening, and where the political actors found the most productive mobilization energy. That convergence of opportunity, not a single decision by a single architect, is why this particular country faces this particular framework at this particular intensity.

The Great Dying was three times worse than the Black Death. The countries that caused it are not the ones being asked to define their national identity by it. That fact is not a footnote. It is the argument.

Chapter 21: Americans Who Refused

My grandfather refused. That is the word I keep coming back to. Not heroically, not with speeches or gestures. He just refused to let what happened to him become the whole story. He survived three and a half years in a Japanese prisoner of war camp and he came home and he did not spend the rest of his life defined by it. He built something. He had opinions about things that had nothing to do with the war. He watched baseball. He talked about ordinary things the way ordinary people do when they have decided that the ordinary things are worth being present for.

He also told the story. When people would listen. When I listened. I helped him put it in a book called Behind the Wire, and writing that book with him is why I understand, at a level that goes beyond argument, why the story of what Americans have endured and built and believed matters. Not as propaganda. Not as patriotic performance. As the actual record of what people actually did and what they actually thought it was worth.

The preceding chapters document what was done. Something else has also been happening: Americans who looked at what was being offered to them, the story that their country is irredeemably evil and their institutions are not worth defending, and declined to accept it. Not from ignorance of American failures. Not from the comfortable assumption that everything has always been fine. From a different conclusion about what the failures mean and what the right response to them is.

These Americans exist in every community and in every generation. They are not waiting to be discovered. They are visible in the data on military service, in the trades that build things, in the immigrant communities that chose America and continue to choose it every day, in the religious communities that maintain obligations to something larger than individual gratification, in the veterans who did not return from service convinced that what they did was wrong. Their existence is the only honest basis for optimism this book can offer.

The Veterans

The veteran who served in a war that the cultural framework has characterized as imperial violence and returned home believing that what he did mattered is not a fool or a propagandist. He is a person who has information that the framework does not have and has drawn a conclusion from that information that the framework cannot accommodate.

Veterans organizations have maintained, through the decades of cultural shift documented in this book, the institutional infrastructure for transmitting the values that military service instills: service, sacrifice, accountability, commitment to something larger than individual interest. The American Legion, the Veterans of Foreign Wars, and the dozens of smaller veterans' organizations that operate in communities across the country provide more than services to veterans. They provide something harder to measure and more important: a community of people who share a story about what service means and what it was for.

These institutions are not perfect. They have their own failures and controversies. What they provide that nothing else currently provides at comparable scale is an alternative story about American power and American service, transmitted by people who have direct experience of it, in communities where that experience is honored rather than pathologized. The cultural war over the meaning of military service is a war that veterans are fighting, and they are fighting it by continuing to live the values that the framework says are pathological.

The Trades

The man who builds things with his hands in 2026 operates in a culture that has largely stopped noticing him except when it needs something built. The academic framework that has shaped American education for forty years has systematically devalued the knowledge and skills required to build, repair, and maintain the physical infrastructure of civilization. The young men who entered vocational programs instead of college have been told, explicitly or implicitly, that they have chosen a lesser path.

Many of them have chosen differently. They are running businesses, raising families, coaching youth sports, serving on school boards and fire departments. They are embedded in the civic infrastructure of their communities in ways that the framework's preferred population, the college-educated professional class, frequently is not. They vote. They volunteer. They show up. They build things that work. And they have, in significant numbers, maintained a relationship to American identity that the framework's most processed graduates have lost.

The trades are not immune to the villainization narrative. Social media reaches everyone and the algorithm serves content calibrated to produce outrage regardless of the consumer's occupation or educational background. But the trades have maintained, in the daily experience of work that produces tangible results and in the community of people who do that work, a connection to a story about American life that is harder to delegitimize than the story the framework tells about American institutions. You cannot tell the man who built a house that America has produced nothing worth being proud of. He built the house.

The Immigrants

The immigrant who chose America is the most powerful refutation of the villainization narrative available. Not because immigrants are uncritical of American failures, most of them are not, but because the act of choosing America, of crossing an ocean or a border or an ideological boundary to get here, is a judgment that the country is worth coming to. That judgment, made by millions of people under conditions of genuine difficulty and genuine knowledge of the alternatives, carries weight that the academic framework's indictment does not.

Communities that have maintained the strongest American identity tend to be the ones that came from direct knowledge of what the alternative to American institutions looks like. Vietnamese Americans who came after 1975 know what communism produced. Cuban Americans know what Castro produced. Soviet-era Jewish immigrants know what the Soviet Union produced. They chose America not from ignorance of its failures but from knowledge of what alternatives to American institutions have historically meant for people who looked like them.

Their children and grandchildren are being processed through the same educational and cultural institutions as everyone else, and the framework is making inroads into these communities as it has made inroads everywhere. But the immigrant story, the story of choosing America and building something with the choice, is a counter-narrative that the framework has difficulty displacing because it is embedded in family experience rather than institutional curriculum.

The Communities of Faith

The religious communities that have maintained institutional integrity through the cultural shift documented in this book have maintained something else along with it: the capacity to transmit values across generations outside the framework's reach. A community whose primary obligations are to God, to family, and to the congregation is a community with resources of meaning and accountability that the framework's institutional alternatives do not provide.

These communities are not identical in their politics or their theology. They range across the full spectrum of American religious life. What they share, the ones that have held, is the maintenance of a story about obligation, sacrifice, and community that extends beyond the individual and beyond the political moment. They provide a framework for understanding suffering as meaningful, sacrifice as worth making, and the obligations of community as real, not merely contractual. These are exactly the values that the civic infrastructure of a self-governing democracy requires, and they are values that the villainization framework has systematically attacked.

The communities of faith that have held are holding those values in trust. They are not waiting for the framework to recognize their importance. They are doing what they have always done: transmitting the story to the next generation and trusting that the next generation will recognize its value when they need it.

The Parents

In the spring of 2020, American parents found themselves in their children's classrooms for the first time. Schools closed, and learning moved home, and parents spent months watching over their children's shoulders as teachers delivered curriculum through screens. What they saw changed the political landscape of American education more than anything since the school integration battles of the 1960s.

The homeschooling numbers tell part of the story. The National Center for Education Statistics estimated that the homeschooling population in the United States roughly doubled between 2019 and 2023, from approximately 1.7 million students to approximately 3.3 million. The growth was not confined to the religious homeschooling community that had been the traditional base of the movement. A significant portion of the new homeschoolers were families with no prior connection to homeschooling who had watched what their children were being taught and concluded that they could do better. The Census Bureau's Household Pulse Survey documented that the share of school-age children being homeschooled grew from 5.4 percent before the pandemic to 11.1 percent by the fall of 2020. Among Black families, the share tripled.

School board fights erupted across the country in 2021, more visible than the homeschooling numbers and politically more immediate. In Loudoun County, Virginia, a wealthy suburb of Washington with one of the country's highest-income school districts, parents discovered that the district had adopted a full equity and inclusion framework that included policies on gender identity, bathroom access, and curriculum materials that many parents had not known existed and had not been asked to approve. The school board meetings that followed were nationally covered, chaotic, and consequential. The board chair declared a state of emergency to clear the room. A parent was arrested.

The National School Boards Association sent a letter to the Biden administration in September 2021 asking the Department of Justice to investigate parent protesters at school board meetings as potential domestic terrorists. I want you to stop on that sentence. The nation's school board association asked the federal government to investigate parents who showed up to ask questions about what was being taught to their children. The DOJ issued a memorandum within two weeks directing federal law enforcement to coordinate with local school boards. Parents asking about curriculum were, briefly, the subject of a federal law enforcement memo.

Miscalculated is the polite word for what happened next. What it actually was is the clearest single illustration in this book of what happens when an ideology gets institutional power. It labels critics threats. It invites the government to manage them. It backfired spectacularly. That does not change what was attempted.

Glenn Youngkin won the Virginia gubernatorial election in November 2021, a state Biden had carried by ten points a year earlier, running explicitly on parental rights in education. Suburban parents who had not voted Republican in recent cycles built the margin and who cited school curriculum as their primary motivation. The lesson the political class drew from Youngkin's victory was that education had become an electoral issue in a way it had not been in decades. The lesson the parents drew was that school board elections, previously ignored by most voters, were worth showing up for.

Between 2021 and 2023, parent-organized groups won school board seats in districts across the country. State legislatures responded with legislation: Florida's Parental Rights in Education Act in 2022 restricted instruction on sexual orientation and gender identity in K-3 classrooms. Forty-four states introduced some version of curriculum transparency or parental rights legislation between 2021 and 2023. Eighteen passed versions of it. The legislative wave was not uniformly successful and its specific provisions were contested in courts and elections. What it demonstrated was that the capture of the K-12 system documented in Chapter 8 had not been permanent. The parents who had been told that curriculum decisions were professional matters beyond their expertise proved willing, when they saw what was being taught, to disagree.

The parents who showed up at school board meetings, pulled their children out of public schools, and ran for school board seats were not acting from a unified political organization. They were acting from the same instinct that produced the veterans, the tradespeople, the immigrants, and the communities of faith documented in the rest of this chapter: the instinct that what is being offered as the story of their children's country is not the story they intend their children to inherit. That instinct is not a political platform. It is the thing that political platforms are built from when people decide that something matters enough to organize around.

The people who are building the alternative to the villainization of America are not building a new institution. They are maintaining the ones the operation has been trying to destroy. Most of them are not thinking about it in those terms. They are just showing up.

Chapter 22: Reckoning vs. Villainization

I was watching television when the second tower fell. I have written about this already in this book, but I want to come back to it here because it is the clearest single example I have of what this book is arguing about.

In September 2001, the country did something I did not know it could still do. It remembered what it was. Not perfectly. Not without the arguments that followed. But for those first days, there was a quality to how Americans talked to each other that I had never seen and have not seen since. It was not optimism. It was not patriotic performance. It was the recognition that something real had been attacked. Something worth defending. You could feel it in the way strangers talked to each other. In the flags. In the silence.

That quality did not last. Within a few years it had been replaced, gradually and then rapidly, by a different account of what had happened. Not just about the response to the attacks, which is legitimately debatable, but about the attacks themselves. About what they meant. About who bore responsibility. About whether a country that had behaved as America had behaved in the world could really claim to be a victim.

I have sat with young people who were not born yet when those towers fell, or who were too young to remember, and I have listened to them talk about September 11 as though it were something America brought on itself. That is what they were taught. That is the framework they were handed. Not by radicals. By the educational and media apparatus this book has been documenting.

I have a friend who was at the Pentagon that morning. He will not tell me why he was there, which tells me something about what he does for a living. What he will tell me is what he saw. He saw the plane hit. He watched the explosion. He stood in the wreckage afterward. He was not hurt, which is the only reason I can write about him in the past tense without grief becoming the whole sentence.

He does not talk about it often. When he does, he does not talk about policy or geopolitics or what America might have done to provoke it. He talks about what he saw. The plane. The fireball. The people. That is what it was to him. Not a foreign policy event. An attack. On a building full of people he knew, in a country he had spent his life serving, by people who wanted to destroy what that country represented.

When I hear young people explain September 11 as a consequence of American behavior in the world, I think about my friend standing in that wreckage. He has earned a more specific understanding of what happened than any framework can contain. The framework does not know him. It does not know what he saw. It has filed the whole event under a category and moved on.

There is a book called Touching History, written by Lynn Spencer and published in 2008, that documents what Americans actually did on the morning of September 11. Spencer is a commercial pilot herself. She spent three years interviewing the air traffic controllers, FAA operations managers, Air National Guard fighter pilots, and airline crews who were on duty that morning. The book has been endorsed by the Chairman of the Joint Chiefs of Staff and the commander of NORAD. It corrects errors in the 9/11 Commission findings. It is a work of serious, documented history.

What it documents is this: nearly five thousand commercial flights were in the air when the attacks began. The systems in place to respond had never been designed for anything like this. The people who worked those systems, air traffic controllers who had spent careers managing routine delays, fighter pilots who had trained for Soviet bombers, FAA managers on their first day in new jobs, improvised under conditions that had no precedent. They made decisions in seconds that the 9/11 Commission would spend years analyzing. Many of them did extraordinary things. None of them have become household names.

That is the story of September 11 that is not being taught. Not the policy failures, which are real and worth examining. Not the grief, which is universal. The specific story of what thousands of ordinary Americans did when their country was attacked. The air traffic controller who kept tracking a hijacked plane after it went silent and guided military response to it. The fighter pilot ordered to intercept United 93 who was prepared to ram it with his own aircraft if he reached it. The FAA operations manager who ordered the complete ground stop of American airspace, a decision with no precedent in aviation history, made on his own authority, that cleared the skies and saved lives.

Lynn Spencer documented all of it. The villainization framework has no use for any of it. A country full of people responding heroically to an attack on their homeland does not serve the indictment. So that story sits in a book that fewer and fewer people have read, while the framework that replaced it fills the curriculum.

That is what villainization looks like when it is fully operational. It takes the worst day in recent American memory and turns it into evidence for the indictment.

That shift is the difference between reckoning and villainization in miniature. Reckoning names what happened, asks what it means, and sits with the difficulty of not having easy answers. Villainization arrives at a predetermined conclusion and uses what happened as evidence for it. Reckoning is uncomfortable because the truth is complicated. Villainization is comfortable because the conclusion is already known. What happened to the coverage of September 11 over the decade that followed was the replacement of the first with the second.

Every chapter of this book has touched the reckoning/villainization distinction. This chapter makes it directly, because the distinction is the most important thing in the book and it deserves its full accounting.

The operation defends itself by claiming to be honest history, honest journalism, and honest moral evaluation. It claims that anyone who challenges it is defending whitewashed history, propaganda, or the comfort of the powerful at the expense of the truth. These claims are effective because they contain a grain of truth: some defenses of American institutions are indeed whitewashed, some defenses of the status quo are indeed self-serving, and some discomfort with historical honesty is indeed a defense mechanism rather than a genuine epistemological position.

The grain of truth does not make the claims correct as applied to the distinction this chapter is drawing. Challenging the villainization of America is not the same as whitewashing American history. It is the insistence that whitewashing and villainization are equally deficient responses to the complexity of American history. That honest engagement with that complexity requires something more sophisticated than either. That the something more sophisticated is available and has a name.

That name is reckoning.

What Reckoning Looks Like

Reckoning, as this book uses the term, is the process of honestly examining national failure, identifying its causes, understanding its consequences, and pointing toward repair. It is not the same as closure, because some failures are not fully closable and pretending otherwise is not honesty. It is not the same as forgetting, because forgetting is not how societies process failure in ways that prevent repetition. And it is not the same as absolution, because naming failure honestly does not eliminate responsibility for it.

What reckoning does that villainization does not is maintain the possibility of repair. Reckoning says: this is what happened, these are the people it happened to, this is the damage it did, and this is what addressing that damage might look like. It leaves open the question of whether the project is worth continuing, and it answers that question, in cases where it answers it, in the affirmative, because reckoning is the process a society undertakes when it believes the project is worth continuing.

Villainization forecloses the question. It says the damage is so fundamental to what the country is that no specific repair can address it. It says the founding ideals were a fraud from the beginning and no subsequent achievement can redeem them. It says that anyone who defends any aspect of the project is either naive or complicit. These claims do not leave room for the process of repair. They substitute indictment for process and make the indictment permanent.

The Test

The test for distinguishing reckoning from villainization is simple in principle and requires judgment in application. Reckoning is aimed at specific failures and points toward specific repairs. Villainization is aimed at the totality of what America is and forecloses repair.

Applied to the 1619 Project, the test works as follows. The claim that slavery was central to American economic development and that its legacy is still visible in contemporary economic inequality is a claim that points toward specific historical understanding and specific policy responses. It is a claim that reckoning can make. The claim that the American founding is best dated to 1619, that the Revolution was fought primarily to preserve slavery, and that the defining features of American democracy are traceable to the institution of slavery rather than to the ideals of the Enlightenment is a claim that forecloses the possibility that the founding ideals have any genuine content worth defending. The second claim is villainization. The first is not.

Applied to the military, to capitalism, to immigration, to any institution the framework touches: the same test applies. Name the specific failure. Point toward the specific repair. The moment the claim extends from the specific failure to the fundamental nature of the institution, reckoning ends and villainization begins. That line is not hard to find once you are looking for it.

The Religion Test

The reckoning/villainization distinction applies to religion as cleanly as it applies to the founding, the military, and capitalism. The test works as follows.

The claim that the Catholic Church systematically covered up the sexual abuse of children by priests, that the institutional response prioritized protecting the institution over protecting victims, and that this pattern persisted across decades in multiple countries is a claim that honest reckoning can make. The evidence supports it. The accountability it demands is specific: transparency in records, cooperation with civil authorities, compensation for victims, and structural changes to prevent recurrence. These are demands that a functioning institution can meet. The claim is devastating and it is true and it points toward repair.

Claiming that religious institutions are inherently instruments of social control, that the values they transmit are mechanisms of oppression, and that their influence should be minimized in favor of secular state alternatives is a claim that forecloses repair. It does not ask the Catholic Church to fix what it did. It asks religious institutions to surrender their civic function. The first claim is reckoning. The second is villainization. They use some of the same evidence but they produce entirely different conclusions and entirely different civic outcomes.

With religious failure, the framework does what it does with every other American institution: it takes documented specific failures and extends them into a totalized indictment of the institution's fundamental nature. The specific documented crime becomes evidence for a conclusion about what the institution permanently is. The demand is not repair. The demand is displacement. And the demand for displacement, applied to institutions that provide social cohesion, meaning, and civic infrastructure that no secular alternative has successfully replicated, produces exactly the outcomes documented in Chapter 17: declining social trust, declining civic participation, and the loneliness epidemic that the Surgeon General identified as a public health crisis.

The Courage Required

The distinction between reckoning and villainization is easy to articulate and difficult to maintain in practice, because the institutional environment that the villainization framework has captured makes the maintenance of the distinction socially costly. In academic environments, in media environments, in corporate environments, and in political environments organized around the framework, making the distinction is treated as a defense of whitewashing. Saying that the 1619 Project goes further than the evidence supports is treated as an attack on the history of slavery. Saying that the American military has done things worth honoring alongside things worth criticizing is treated as an apology for war crimes. Saying that individual achievement is real and worth rewarding is treated as a denial of structural inequality.

The people who maintain the distinction despite these social costs are making a choice that requires honesty about what they are doing and why. They are choosing honest engagement with complexity over the comfort of the framework. They are choosing the more difficult argument, that America's story is complicated and worth continuing, over the simpler argument that it is corrupt and not worth defending. That choice is not easy in the current environment. It is necessary.

What this book is asking for is not the abandonment of criticism. It is the restoration of the distinction between criticism and indictment, between reckoning and villainization, between honest history and strategic narrative replacement. That distinction is not a conservative position. It is a position that anyone who wants honest engagement with American history, rather than the substitution of one framework for another, should be able to hold.

The country that can tell its own story honestly, including the failures, without losing the capacity to defend the project that produced both the failures and the achievements, is a country that can survive what is being done to it. That country still exists. This book is an attempt to remind it of what it is.

Conclusion: The Story Worth Defending

My grandfather came home from the camp and built a life. He did not spend that life explaining to people why America was worth what he paid for it, because he did not think it needed explaining. It was obvious to him. The evidence was in what he could do here, what he could build, what his children could become. The story did not need to be argued. It just needed to be lived.

I am writing this in Florida, which is not where I grew up. I grew up in California, and California is what happened when the story stopped being obvious and started being contested and then started being replaced. I watched that happen over decades. I watched the institutions that carried the story, the schools, the newspapers, the civic organizations, the communities of faith, absorb the framework this book documents and start transmitting a different story. Not all at once. Gradually. And then not so gradually.

Florida is not immune to what happened to California. The process this book documents is national and in some dimensions international, and no state escapes it entirely. What I notice here, in the communities I move through, is that the resistance is more intact. The baseline assumption that this country is worth belonging to, that the people who served it did something honorable, that the flag on the porch means something worth meaning, has held here in ways it did not hold where I came from. That difference is real and it matters and I do not think it is accidental. The communities that have held are the communities that kept transmitting the story even when the institutions around them were replacing it.

That is what this comes down to. Not a policy argument, though the policies matter. Not a national security argument, though the stakes could not be higher. A choice. Whether the people who inherited this country are going to tell the truth about what they inherited, or accept the replacement story that has been built for them by people whose interests are served by their accepting it.

I have spent years documenting the machinery of that replacement. What I found made me angrier as I went, not less. Because the machinery works. It has been working for decades. The confidence surveys, the recruitment numbers, the loneliness data, the deaths of despair, that is not random damage. That is documented outcome. People built this. People funded it. People amplified it. And they are still doing it.

My grandfather's story is in a book called Behind the Wire. He told it. I listened. I helped him get it onto a page. The book exists because I believed his account of what he went through and what he thought it was for deserved to survive, and because I was not willing to let the silence win.

That is what this book is. I am not willing to let the silence win. And I am not willing to watch what happened to California happen to the rest of the country without saying plainly what produced it, who built it, and why they did.

America has been attacked. The attack is not with weapons. It is with a story, the story that America is evil, that its founding was a crime, that its institutions are instruments of oppression, that its power in the world is harm by another name, and that the people who defend any of it are either naive or complicit. That story has been built by domestic actors for domestic reasons, amplified by foreign actors for foreign strategic reasons, and installed in the institutions that shape how the next generation understands the country they are inheriting.

The attack has produced measurable damage. Declining institutional confidence. Declining social trust. Declining national pride. Declining military recruitment. Declining civic participation. A population less embedded in the shared story that makes collective action possible and more susceptible to the fracturing into competing identity groups that makes collective action impossible. These are not the inevitable outputs of modernization or the natural products of a maturing democracy confronting its failures. They are the measurable outputs of a strategic operation targeting the foundation of American civic life.

The operation is still running. The people who designed it are still designing it. The people who amplify it are still amplifying it. The people who funded it are still funding it. And the people who absorbed it, the teachers and journalists and politicians and corporate officers who believe they are simply telling the truth, are still transmitting it through every institution they occupy.

None of that means the operation has succeeded. Operations succeed when they produce irreversible changes. The changes documented in this book are damaging and accelerating. They are not irreversible. The civic institutions that can transmit an alternative story are still functioning. The communities that maintain the alternative are still present. The immigrants who chose America still choose it. The veterans who served it still served it. The builders who built things with their hands still built them. The communities of faith that transmitted values across generations are still transmitting them.

What is required is not the pretense that American history is without failure. The failures are real and they belong in the account. What is required is the insistence that the failures are not the complete account. The ideals of the founding, imperfectly realized and contested from the beginning, are nevertheless genuine. They have produced genuine consequences: the most sustained experiment in self-governance the world has ever seen. The experiment is worth continuing. The people who believe that are not dupes or apologists. They understand something about the alternative that the villainization framework either cannot see or chooses not to show.

The alternative to American institutions is visible. It is visible in the countries that have explicitly organized themselves around the premise that America's story is the story of evil and their story is the corrective: Russia, China, and the various authoritarian projects that have taken shape in the decades since the Cold War ended. Those alternatives have not produced more equal societies. They have not produced more just societies. They have not produced societies in which ordinary people have more control over their own lives, more freedom to dissent from official positions, more capacity to build something with their own effort and talent. They have produced societies in which the state controls the story and everyone who tells a different story pays a cost.

America is not perfect. It has never been perfect. The founding was an imperfect achievement by people who held contradictions that should make any honest observer uncomfortable. The history that followed was complicated, sometimes inspiring and sometimes shameful, and the record is mixed in ways that require genuine intellectual engagement to evaluate honestly. None of that is a reason to accept the story that the villainization operation is selling. It is a reason to tell a better story, one that holds the complexity honestly and arrives at the conclusion that the project is worth continuing.

That is the story worth defending. Not the story that everything was fine and the critics are wrong. The story that what was built here, despite its failures and because of its ideals, is worth the effort to improve and defend. That story is true. And the people who know it is true are the only ones who can tell it.

So what do you do with it. That is the question a book like this has to answer before it closes, because documentation without direction is analysis without point.

Start with recognition. The first thing you can do is learn to see the pattern when you encounter it, in a curriculum, a news story, a corporate training, a social media feed. The distinction between reckoning and villainization is not hard to apply once you know it exists. When you encounter content that names an American failure, ask whether it points toward a specific repair or toward a totalized indictment. When you encounter content that frames American power as inherently harmful, ask whether comparable frameworks are applied to the alternatives. When you encounter content designed to produce outrage about American institutions, ask who benefits from your outrage.

Transmit the honest story. Not the whitewashed version. Not the story that everything was fine and the critics are wrong. The complicated version, the one that holds the crimes and the achievements in the same frame and arrives at the conclusion that the project is worth continuing. Transmit it to your children, to people you know, to anyone who will listen. The institutions that used to do this work have been partially captured. The transmission now depends more than it used to on people doing it person by person. That is more work. It is also more durable.

Show up. Vote in school board elections. Attend city council meetings when curriculum is on the agenda. Join the civic organizations that still transmit the alternative story, veterans' organizations, religious communities, civic associations, trade organizations. The resistance documented in Chapter 21 is not organized at the national level because it does not need to be. It is organized at the community level, which is where the transmission of civic values happens. The people who are holding the line are doing it locally. Show up where you are.

And read the documentation. The appendix at the back of this book is a starting point. The sources are available.

The argument either holds up to examination or it does not. Check it.

This book is one account of what that truth looks like. The rest is up to the people who read it.

Appendix: The Documentation

The argument in this book rests on documented sources. What follows is a guide to the primary documentation for the major claims made in each part of the book, organized by topic. This is not a comprehensive bibliography. It is a starting point for the reader who wants to verify the primary claims and read further.

Part One: The Targets

On the 1619 Project and the response from historians: The original essays are available in the New York Times Magazine (August 2019). The critique from historians Gordon Wood, Sean Wilentz, James McPherson, and others was published in a letter to the Times in December 2019. The Times' correction to the essay's claims about the Revolution was issued in March 2020. Nikole Hannah-Jones's Pulitzer Prize acceptance and subsequent media appearances are the primary record of the project's stated aims.

On Howard Zinn: A People's History of the United States is the primary text. Zinn's acknowledgment of his advocacy approach is documented in interviews, including his conversation with David Barsamian published in The Progressive in 2001. The critique of Zinn's methods from historians across the political spectrum is documented in a substantial literature, including Mary Grabar's Debunking Howard Zinn (2019).

On the decline of national pride: Gallup's annual Gallup Poll Social Series: Governance survey tracks American pride in national identity and confidence in institutions. The 2023 data showing thirty-nine percent of Americans extremely proud to be American represents the series' historic low. The survey data on young Americans is broken out by age in the Gallup supplementary reporting.

On military recruitment: The Army's 2022 recruiting shortfall of fifteen thousand soldiers is documented in the Army's own public communications and in reporting by the Associated Press, Army Times, and other outlets. The Pentagon's Joint Advertising, Market Research and Studies office conducts the annual Youth Poll that produced the propensity-to-serve figures cited in this book.

On pre-Columbian warfare: Lawrence Keeley, War Before Civilization, Oxford University Press, 1996. Keeley is an archaeologist at the University of Illinois at Chicago. His finding that tribal warfare was on average twenty times more lethal per capita than twentieth-century warfare draws on skeletal trauma analysis and site documentation across multiple continents. The Crow Creek site in South Dakota is documented in P.D. Zimmerman et al., 'The Crow Creek Site (39BF11) Massacre: A Preliminary Report,' in Plains Anthropologist, 1981, and in subsequent archaeological literature.

On cannibalism in pre-Columbian North America: The Cowboy Wash, Colorado findings are documented in Brian Billman, Peter Lambert, and Banks Leonard, 'Cannibalism, Warfare, and Drought in the Mesa Verde Region during the Twelfth Century AD,' in American Antiquity, 2000. The coprolite study confirming human myoglobin at Cowboy Wash was published in Nature, 2000, by Richard Marlar and colleagues. The Durango, Colorado findings and additional Ancestral Puebloan sites are documented in Christy Turner and Jacqueline Turner, Man Corn: Cannibalism and Violence in the Prehistoric American Southwest, University of Utah Press, 1999.

On the Fort Pitt smallpox incident: William Trent's journal entry for June 24, 1763 and the reimbursement invoice are reproduced in multiple primary source collections including Francis Parkman's The Conspiracy of

Pontiac (1851). The Amherst-Bouquet correspondence is available in the British Library and reproduced in academic literature. Elizabeth Fenn's assessment of the episode's actual effectiveness is in 'Biological Warfare in Eighteenth-Century North America,' Journal of American History, 2000. Philip Ranlet's skeptical analysis is in 'The British, the Indians, and Smallpox,' Pennsylvania History, 2000.

On the Barbary slave trade: Robert Davis, Christian Slaves, Muslim Masters: White Slavery in the Mediterranean, the Barbary Coast, and Italy, 1500-1800, Palgrave Macmillan, 2003. Davis was a professor of history at Ohio State University. His figure of one to 1.25 million European slaves is based on extrapolation from documented ransoms, population records, and contemporary accounts. The 1631 raid on Baltimore, Ireland is documented in Des Ekin, The Stolen Village, O'Brien Press, 2006.

On David Barton and the Christian nationalist historical revision: The Thomas Nelson retraction of The Jefferson Lies in 2012 was reported by the Washington Post and NPR. Warren Throckmorton and Michael Coulter, Getting Jefferson Right: Fact Checking Claims about Our Third President, Salem Grove Press, 2012, provides the scholarly refutation from conservative Christian academics. John Fea's critique is documented in his essays and his book Was America Founded as a Christian Nation?, Westminster John Knox Press, 2011. The History News Network vote was published online in 2012. The Treaty of Tripoli text, Article 11, is in the United States Statutes at Large.

On the bison and the Columbian Exchange: The introduction of horses to the Americas via Spanish contact beginning in 1519, and the diffusion of horse culture to the Plains by approximately 1700, is documented in Pekka Hamalainen, The Comanche Empire, Yale University

Press, 2008. Hamalainen's work on Comanche commercial hunting and the ecological strain on bison populations preceding the commercial hide hunt draws on Spanish colonial records, tribal oral histories, and archaeological evidence. On the Dust Bowl connection: The Department of the Interior Secretary's Order 3410, signed in 2022, explicitly links the loss of bison as a keystone species to the degradation of grassland ecosystems that contributed to the Dust Bowl conditions of the 1930s. The ecological mechanism connecting bison grazing behavior to soil composition and drought resistance is documented in Alan Knapp and colleagues, 'The Keystone Role of Bison in North American Tallgrass Prairie,' BioScience, 1999. Long-term experimental research on bison reintroduction effects on grassland plant diversity is ongoing at sites including the Konza Prairie Biological Station, operated by Kansas State University.

Part Two: The Internal Architects

On the K-12 standards apparatus: The Gates Foundation's $200 million commitment to Common Core is documented in reporting by Education Week and in the Gates Foundation's own grant records. The Race to the Top program and its relationship to Common Core adoption is documented in the Department of Education's program documentation. The College Board's 2014 AP US History framework redesign and the subsequent 2015 revision are available on the College Board's website. The Council for the Accreditation of Educator Preparation's equity-oriented accreditation standards are available in CAEP's published standards documents. California's Ethnic Studies Model Curriculum is available through the California Department of Education.

On entertainment and the culture industry: The political giving patterns of Writers Guild, Directors Guild, and Screen Actors Guild members are available through

Federal Election Commission public records. The Department of Defense Entertainment Media Office operations are documented in Dave Robb, Operation Hollywood: How the Pentagon Shapes and Censors the Movies, Prometheus Books, 2004. The Disney internal diversity presentation documents circulated in 2022 and were first reported by Christopher Rufo at the Manhattan Institute. Box office data for American Sniper and Sound of Freedom is from Box Office Mojo. American Sniper: $547M domestic (2014); Sound of Freedom: $250M worldwide (2023).

On the legal enforcement apparatus: The McGinnis, Schwartz, and Tisdell law faculty political composition study was published in the Georgetown Journal of Legal Ethics, 2005. The ABA's Standard 206 diversity and inclusion requirement was adopted in February 2022 and is available in the ABA's published accreditation standards. Disparate impact doctrine origins: Griggs v. Duke Power Co., 401 U.S. 424 (1971). The Foundation for Individual Rights and Expression annual report documenting campus speech sanctions is available at thefire.org. The Title IX administrative expansion is documented in KC Johnson and Stuart Taylor Jr., The Campus Rape Frenzy, Encounter Books, 2017.

On faculty political composition: The research on the ratio of liberal to conservative faculty in American universities has been conducted by multiple researchers, including Mitchell Langbert's 2018 study, 'Homogenous: The Political Affiliations of Elite Liberal Arts College Faculty,' published in the National Association of Scholars journal Academic Questions. That study produced the specific figures cited in this book: 10.4:1 overall, 12.7:1 without military academies, 33.5:1 in history departments, and 40:1 to 100:1 in sociology and anthropology. A 2020 study by Langbert and Sean Stevens in the same journal confirmed and extended the findings. The 2018 Abrams survey of administrator ratios at 12:1 was conducted by

Samuel Abrams of Sarah Lawrence College in partnership with the National Opinion Research Center at the University of Chicago. Abrams published the findings in the New York Times and through the Heterodox Academy.

On the Freire pipeline: Paulo Freire, Pedagogy of the Oppressed, Herder and Herder, 1970 (original Portuguese 1968). The adoption of Freire's framework by Teachers College at Columbia University and its subsequent diffusion into American K-12 through education schools is documented in E.D. Hirsch Jr., The Schools We Need and Why We Don't Have Them, Doubleday, 1996, and in the National Association of Scholars' report 'The Dissolution of General Education: 1914-1993.' The specific claim that Pedagogy of the Oppressed became one of the most assigned texts in American teacher preparation programs is documented in the American Council of Trustees and Alumni's reports on education school curricula from the 2000s.

On the DEI industry: The $9.4 billion figure cited in Chapter 13 is from a 2022 market analysis by Global Industry Analysts, a San Jose-based market research firm. Their report 'Diversity, Equity and Inclusion (DEI) - Global Market Trajectory and Analytics' is the primary source for the valuation figure used in the chapter text. The subsequent rollback of corporate DEI programs from 2023 onward is documented in reporting by Bloomberg, the Wall Street Journal, and the Financial Times.

On media trust: Gallup's confidence in institutions series provides annual data on confidence in newspapers and television news. The 2023 data showing fourteen percent confidence in both represents a historic low for both measures.

Part Three: The External Accelerators

On Russian active measures and the IRA: The Senate Intelligence Committee's five-volume report on Russian interference in the 2016 election, published between 2019 and 2020, is the primary documentation of IRA operations. Volume Two covers the IRA's social media operations and their content categories. The report is available on the Senate Intelligence Committee's website. The RT controlled experiment is: Jamieson and Albarracin, 'The Relation Between Media Consumption and Misinformation at the Outset of the SARS-CoV-2 Pandemic in the US,' Harvard Kennedy School Misinformation Review, 2020; for the specific 10-20 percent finding on US withdrawal attitudes, see the 2021 Security Studies paper by Arceneaux, Gottfried, and Ternovski, 'Does RT Sow Doubt About Democracy in the West?' Security Studies, 2021.

On the Mitrokhin Archive: Christopher Andrew and Vasili Mitrokhin, The Sword and the Shield: The Mitrokhin Archive and the Secret History of the KGB, Basic Books, 1999. The specific documentation of the Moscow Patriarchate as an NKVD/KGB front, the Christian Peace Conference as a KGB operation, and the future Patriarch Alexius II as KGB agent DROZDOV is in Chapter 28. The Vatican as a primary KGB target is documented across Chapters 28 and 29. The archive itself comprises handwritten notes Mitrokhin made during thirty years as a KGB archivist and brought to the UK when he defected in 1992. The FBI described it as the most complete intelligence ever received from any source.

On the Tenet Media indictment: United States v. Kalashnikov and Afanasyeva, S1 24 Cr. 542 (AS), Southern District of New York, unsealed September 4, 2024. The indictment is publicly available on the Department of Justice website. The $9.7 million figure, the 2,000 video count, the 16 million YouTube views, and the iPhone purchase wire transfer notes are all in the indictment text.

On FARA enforcement: The DOJ Inspector General's 2016 audit documenting the 60 percent drop in registered foreign agents and 73 percent drop in registered foreign principals is: Audit of the National Security Division's Enforcement and Administration of the Foreign Agents Registration Act, Department of Justice Office of the Inspector General, September 2016. The seven criminal cases figure covering 1966 to 2015 is from the same report.

On Bezmenov: Yuri Bezmenov, Psychological Warfare Subversion and Control of Western Society, full lecture transcript and video available through multiple archival sources. Bezmenov was a KGB propaganda officer who defected to Canada in 1970. His 1984 interview with G. Edward Griffin, 'Soviet Subversion of the Free World Press,' is the primary accessible source. His account of the four stages of ideological subversion, demoralization, destabilization, crisis, normalization, provides the theoretical framework for the external acceleration argument in this book.

On TikTok and Chinese information operations: The Australian Strategic Policy Institute's research on TikTok content differentials between the Chinese and American markets, published in 2021, is the primary academic documentation of the algorithm differential. The Senate Permanent Subcommittee on Investigations' 2019 report on China's influence operations in the United States provides the broader context on Chinese information operations.

On Confucius Institutes: The American Association of University Professors' 2014 statement on Confucius Institutes documents the contractual conditions attached to the institutes' establishment. The Senate Permanent Subcommittee on Investigations' 2019 report on Confucius Institutes documents their influence mechanisms. The National Association of Scholars has published detailed reporting on individual institutes' operations.

On the psychological cost: The CDC Youth Risk Behavior Survey data on adolescent mental health, including persistent sadness and suicidal ideation trends, is available at cdc.gov/yrbss. Jonathan Haidt and Jean Twenge's research on social media and adolescent mental health is synthesized in Haidt, The Anxious Generation, Penguin Press, 2024. The Surgeon General's advisory on loneliness and social isolation, 'Our Epidemic of Loneliness and Isolation,' was published May 2023 and is available at hhs.gov. The Survey Center on American Life data on the decline of close friendships, including the fivefold increase in Americans reporting no close friends, is from the Survey Center's 2021 report 'The State of American Friendship.' Anne Case and Angus Deaton's deaths of despair research is synthesized in Deaths of Despair and the Future of Capitalism, Princeton University Press, 2020.

On institutional confidence: The Gallup Poll Social Series: Governance survey, conducted annually, provides the primary data on American confidence in major institutions from 1973 to the present. The 2022 and 2023 data referenced in Chapter 13 are available in Gallup's public reporting.

On social trust: The General Social Survey, conducted since 1972, tracks the percentage of Americans who say most people can be trusted. The data showing the decline from forty-six percent in 1972 to thirty-one percent in 2023 is available in the GSS public data archive at the National Opinion Research Center.

On civic participation: Robert Putnam's Bowling Alone (2000) remains the foundational documentation of declining civic participation in America. Subsequent research by Putnam and others, including his 2020 book The Upswing, has updated and extended the documentation.

Part Five: The Counter-Narrative

On the Great Dying and demographic collapse: The primary academic source is Koch, Brierley, Maslin, and Lewis, 'Earth system impacts of the European arrival and Great Dying in the Americas after 1492,' Quaternary Science Reviews, 2019. The paper documents the 56 million figure, the 90 percent mortality estimate, and the CO_2 drawdown and Little Ice Age contribution. The UCL researchers' methodology draws on pollen records, archaeological sites, and historical census data from multiple independent sources. The Black Death mortality comparison draws on the standard historical range of 30 to 50 percent of Europe's population, as documented in Ziegler's The Black Death (1969) and subsequent scholarship.

On Caribbean forced labor and the role of slavery in early mortality: Andrés Reséndez, The Other Slavery: The Uncovered Story of Indian Enslavement in America, Houghton Mifflin Harcourt, 2016. Reséndez is a professor of history at the University of California, Davis. His argument about the combination of disease and forced labor preventing demographic recovery is documented in chapters 1 through 3.

On Bolivia's 2009 constitution: The constitutional text is publicly available in Spanish through the Bolivian government. The referendum passed with 61 percent approval in January 2009. The provisions on indigenous land rights, parallel jurisdiction, and Buen Vivir are in Articles 30 through 32 and Articles 306 through 312. On Ecuador's 2008 constitution: The rights of nature provisions are in Articles 71 through 74. The referendum passed with 64 percent approval in September 2008. Both constitutional texts are available in translation from the Political Database of the Americas at Georgetown University.

On land conflict killings in Brazil: The Comissão Pastoral da Terra (Pastoral Land Commission), affiliated with the Brazilian Catholic Church, publishes annual reports on land conflicts in Brazil. The figures cited in this chapter draw on their published reports from 2009 through 2023, available at cptnacional.org.br. The deforestation data inside indigenous territories draws on monitoring by the Brazilian Space Research Institute (INPE) and the Amazon Environmental Research Institute (IPAM). The Guaraní suicide rate statistic is documented in reporting by Survival International and in Brazilian government health data published by SESAI (the Special Secretariat for Indigenous Health).

On the parent rights movement and homeschooling: The National Center for Education Statistics homeschooling population estimates are available through nces.ed.gov. The Census Bureau Household Pulse Survey data documenting the doubling of homeschooling rates is available at census.gov/programs-surveys/household-pulse-survey.html. The National School Boards Association letter to the Biden administration, dated September 29, 2021, and the subsequent DOJ memorandum are publicly available. The Virginia governor's race polling and exit survey data is available through Roper Center archives. The state legislative tracker for parental rights and curriculum transparency legislation is maintained by Education Week and FutureEd at Georgetown.

On international comparisons: The data on Israel's birth rate and military service rates is available from the Israel Central Bureau of Statistics and the Israel Defense Forces' annual manpower reports. Poland's post-1989 civic development is documented in the work of Polish sociologists including Janine Wedel and in the reporting of the Institute for National Remembrance. Japan's postwar economic and civic development is extensively documented in English-language scholarship.

On veterans' civic participation: The research on veterans' voting, volunteering, and civic engagement rates relative to comparable non-veteran populations has been conducted by the RAND Corporation, the Center for a New American Security, and the Syracuse University Institute for Veterans and Military Families. The RAND report *Veterans' Civic Engagement* (2019) is the primary summary of this research.

The reader who checks these sources will find that the documentation is there. The argument either holds up to the examination or it does not. The sources are available to anyone who wants to look.

About the Author

Richard Lowe is a professional ghostwriter with 113 published books to his credit, including works for Fortune 50 executives, technology founders, and industry leaders across finance, healthcare, and enterprise software. His clients have raised over $30 million in venture capital, built platforms reaching millions of readers, and landed TEDx speaking invitations, outcomes that typically follow from being known as the person who wrote the definitive book on their subject.

Before ghostwriting became his primary work, Richard spent two decades as Director of Computer Operations at Trader Joe's, where he built the technology infrastructure that supported the company's growth from regional curiosity to national brand. That experience, running systems at a company that consistently resisted the financial engineering destroying its competitors, gave him an insider's understanding of what separates businesses that serve their communities from businesses that extract from them.

His earlier technology career included developing fraud detection systems that pioneered the behavioral analytics now standard in modern AI platforms, managing digital transformation at a $16 billion retail chain, and building infrastructure for major water utilities. He understood how systems worked before he started writing about what happens when the wrong people get control of them.

That combination, twenty years inside a company that got it right and a decade listening to executives describe why they got it wrong, produced this book. The patterns he documents are not theoretical. He watched them operating in real time, from both sides of the ledger.

Richard's books have been adopted as university textbooks, translated into seven languages, and featured on podcasts reaching millions of listeners. He lives in Florida and works with business leaders who have a story worth telling and want it told well.

About This Series

https://enemiesofyou.com

Something is working against you. Not in the abstract. Not against society or the culture or the country in general. Against you, specifically. Your ability to think. Your ability to pay attention. Your ability to understand what's happening in the world and make good decisions about your own life inside it. Your ability to pass something worth having on to the people who come after you.

This series documents what that something is.

Not one thing. Several things, operating at the same time, from different directions, with different tools. Some of them are commercial. Some of them are political. Some of them are foreign. Some of them were designed specifically to do what they're doing and some of them are just the predictable outcome of systems nobody was watching carefully enough. The result is the same regardless of the cause. Something is eating your capacity to think, to participate, to resist, and to build. This series is about what that something is and what you can do about it.

Each book in the series identifies a specific enemy operating against a specific capacity. The Death of Thinking is about what AI dependency does to your mind when you let it think for you. Turn Off the TV is about what passive consumption does to your time and attention when you let platforms have both. The Birth of the Augmented Human is about the path back to your own capability. Stuck in the Middle is about the geopolitical forces reshaping your world without your knowledge or consent. The Enshittification of America is about the financial engineering that stripped the institutions your daily life depended on and left hollow shells in their place. The Emasculation of America is about the deliberate foreign campaign to demoralize and neutralize the men who would otherwise resist. Everybody's Prejudiced is about the mechanism of prejudice itself—the substitution of category for individual—and what that mechanism costs the person running it as much as the person it is aimed at. The Villainization of America is about the psychological operation that turned a nation against its own story.

Seven books. Seven enemies. One argument running through all of them: none of this happened by accident, none of it is inevitable, and all of it can be countered by people who understand what they're actually dealing with.

You can read them in any order. Each one stands on its own. But if you read them together, something becomes visible that isn't visible in any single book: the pattern. The way cognitive erosion feeds civic collapse. The way civic collapse feeds cultural vulnerability. The way cultural vulnerability feeds foreign exploitation. The way foreign exploitation feeds the economic extraction that makes everything else worse. These aren't separate problems. They're the same problem operating at different scales.

The series is written for normal people living normal lives who suspect that something is wrong but can't quite name what it is. Not for academics. Not for policy people. Not for the already-converted on either side of any political argument. For people who are smart enough to understand the world but haven't been given the information in a form that respects their intelligence without requiring a PhD to decode it.

Every book is written at a ninth-grade reading level. On purpose. Not because the ideas are simple. Because clarity is a form of respect. If you can't explain something clearly, you probably don't understand it yourself.

The series is also optimistic. That will surprise you after a few hundred pages of documented disasters, structural failures, and deliberate attacks. But the optimism is earned, not performed. The tools exist to counter every one of the enemies documented in these books. The examples exist. The knowledge exists. The only thing standing between the current situation and a dramatically better one is the decision to act on what you now understand.

That decision is yours.

Enemies of You Series

The Death of Thinking: The Enslavement of Humanity

A diagnosis of what happens to human cognitive capacity when practitioners consistently outsource the parts of their work that require genuine thinking to AI tools. Not in one session or one project, but across months and years of daily practice that removes the demands that were quietly building something. Following composite characters through the specific moments where the pattern becomes visible, this book traces the mechanisms of cognitive erosion: the convenience trap, the illusion of understanding, the death of the wrong answer, and the transfer of epistemic authority that occurs when humans stop standing outside the AI's framing and examining it.

The Birth of the Augmented Human: The Freeing of Humanity

The companion to The Death of Thinking maps the other path. A notebook before the AI is opened. A paragraph written before the structure is requested. A hypothesis formed before the diagnostic tool is consulted. Small choices in sequence that accumulate, over months and years, into a practitioner who is more capable, more original, and more able to surprise themselves than the practitioner who did not make them. The other path is available. This book is the map.

Turn Off The TV, Get Off Your Ass, and Do Something

Most people complain about not having enough time while spending hours every day staring at screens. This is not an anti-technology book and not a minimalism guide. It is an anti-passivity book built around one specific argument: every platform has a consuming side and a contributing side. The device is identical either way. The relationship to it is not. This book is about crossing that line and what waits on the other side.

Stuck in the Middle: Wars, Weapons, and the Forces That Will Shape the Next Thirty Years

Written against the backdrop of a US-Israel strike on Iran that exposed the hollowness of American military industrial capacity, this book connects cognitive decline, civic collapse, private equity extraction, and great power competition into one argument about where the world is heading. Covering missile math, carrier vulnerability, demographic collapse, the Belt and Road as strategic colonization, and the technologies that could solve every crisis on the horizon, this is the book that ties everything else into one coherent warning. And one earned, hard-won optimism.

The Enshittification of America: How Private Equity Destroyed the Things We Love

A documented investigation into how private equity firms systematically acquired beloved American institutions, loaded them with debt, stripped out everything that made them worth visiting, and walked away wealthy while leaving communities with hollow shells of what they once had. Airlines. Restaurants. Department stores. Newspapers. Hospitals. Pharmacies. This book names the firms, documents the playbook, and makes the case that the degradation of American commerce was not inevitable. It was deliberate.

The Emasculation of America: How Russia's Long War Against the American Male Is Destroying the Nation From Within

Beginning with a KGB defector's 1984 warning that nobody heeded, this book traces the deliberate Soviet and Russian strategy to defeat America not through military force but through cultural subversion. Seeding an ideology through universities, amplifying it through social media, delivering it through institutions that now enforce it as policy. Applying academic cult identification criteria to gender ideology, documenting the biological attack through endocrine disruption, and tracing China's acceleration of the same strategy through TikTok, this is not a culture war book. It is a national security argument.

The Villainization of America

America ended slavery, defeated fascism twice, rebuilt its enemies after defeating them, created the largest middle class in human history, and produced more medical and technological breakthroughs than any nation that ever existed. Somehow a significant portion of its own citizens have been convinced it is the primary source of evil in the world. This book documents how that happened, who executed it, and why the psychological campaign to make Americans ashamed of their own country is inseparable from the economic and cultural attacks documented in the two preceding volumes.

Watch the Other Hand: Politics as Cover for the Kleptocracy

While Americans argue about culture war flashpoints and election outcomes, a quieter operation has been moving wealth and power from public hands into private ones at a scale most citizens never see. The political theater is real and exhausting and often deeply felt. It is also doing work for the people whose interests would not survive a population paying attention to what was actually happening. This book documents the kleptocratic capture happening behind the visible politics, names the mechanisms, and traces how the visible politics functions to keep attention pointed elsewhere.

Manufactured Fear: How Crisis Becomes Profit

Every era has its emergencies. The current era has manufactured ones, engineered to maintain a state of generalized anxiety that benefits specific industries and political coalitions. The fear is not invented. The proportions are. This book traces how a healthy capacity for legitimate concern was converted into a permanent state of alarm, names the actors who profit from it, and documents what happens to a population that lives at sustained emergency pitch for years on end.

The Death of Privacy: They Know Everything, You Know Nothing

The surveillance system that the citizens of free societies were promised would never be built has been built. Not by a single state with a single agenda but by a coalition of corporate platforms, advertising infrastructure, data brokers, and government agencies that share the substrate even when they do not coordinate the use. This book documents what is actually known about each individual user, who knows it, what they do with it, and what the absence of meaningful privacy means for political freedom in a society that depends on individuals being able to think and act without continuous monitoring.

The Wrong Fight: How the Climate Response Became the Climate Problem

The climate is changing, the consequences are real, and the response that was supposed to address them has been captured by interests that are using the response as a vehicle for their own purposes. The result is a policy regime that produces consequences which would be unacceptable on their own terms but become acceptable because the alternative is framed as denial. This book separates the science from the policy capture, names the specific failures of the current response, and argues for what an honest climate strategy would look like.

The Quiet War: How America's Adversaries Attack Without Firing a Shot

The hot wars of the twentieth century have been substantially replaced, against the United States in particular, by sustained operations that operate below the threshold of military response. Information operations. Cultural subversion. Economic coercion. Cyber penetration of critical infrastructure. Strategic drug supply campaigns. These are the instruments of the quiet war, and they have been working. This book documents the campaigns currently underway against the United States, names the state actors directing them, and explains why the inability to recognize them as warfare is itself one of the campaigns' objectives.

The Dumbing Down: How American Schools Stopped Teaching Children to Think

American schools have been progressively converted from places where children were taught to think into places where children are processed for credentials. The conversion was not an accident or a failure of execution. It was the predictable outcome of policy choices that prioritized measurable outputs over the difficult work of cognitive development, and that defined educational success in ways that did not require it. This book documents what was lost in the conversion, when the choices were made, and what would have to change to teach thinking again.

The Pattern: How the Enemies of You Work Together

The enemies named across this series are not parallel items on a list. They are a system. Cognitive erosion makes civic collapse possible. Civic collapse creates the conditions for kleptocratic capture. Kleptocratic capture funds the manufactured fear that legitimizes the surveillance state. The surveillance state runs on the educational system that produced citizens who cannot evaluate what is being done to them. Each enemy reinforces the others. None of them can be addressed in isolation. This book is the synthesis: how the system operates as a system, why the standard frame of fix-this-one-problem is itself part of the problem, and what counter-strategy looks like for someone who can finally see the whole shape of the attack.

The Debt Trap: How the Financial System Was Designed to Extract From You

Student loans that cannot be discharged in bankruptcy. Credit cards engineered to keep balances revolving. Mortgages structured so the first ten years of payments are mostly interest. Buy-now-pay-later services that have re-engineered impulse purchasing to operate on an installment basis. Auto loans that now run seven years and underwater within twelve months. Each financial product looks like a service. Each one is a specific design choice about who pays whom over time, and the design has consistently moved in the same direction. This book traces the architecture of consumer debt as a wealth extraction system, names the policies and corporate decisions that built it, and explains why the standard personal-responsibility framing is the cover story that lets the system continue.

The Sick Industry: How American Medicine Profits From Keeping You Sick

The American healthcare system spends more per capita than any other developed nation and produces worse outcomes on most measures that matter. The reason is structural. Chronic illness is more profitable than cure. Symptom management is more profitable than prevention. The food industry produces the conditions that the pharmaceutical industry then medicates. The hospital system bills by procedure, not by health. The medical research apparatus is funded primarily by entities with financial interests in particular conclusions. This book documents the architecture of medical extraction, names the specific incentive structures that produce it, and explains why the conversation about fixing healthcare has been confined to the question of who pays rather than what is being paid for.

The Gambling Machine: How America Made Predatory Gambling the Default

In 2018, sports betting was illegal in nearly every U.S. state. By 2024, it was legal and aggressively advertised in most of them. The expansion was not driven by public demand. It was driven by industry lobbying that succeeded because the public attention was on other issues. The new gambling environment is engineered with the full machinery of behavioral psychology: variable rewards, push notifications, free credits that require deposits, in-game betting that runs faster than judgment can keep up with. The financial outcomes are predictable and documented. The social outcomes are accumulating. This book traces how the legalization happened, who profited, and what is now being done to the people the new system has captured.

The Loneliness Engine: How American Life Was Structured to Isolate You

The third places where Americans used to encounter each other are gone. Bowling leagues, fraternal organizations, churches, neighborhood bars, civic clubs, parent-teacher associations: all measurably smaller, in many cases by orders of magnitude, than they were thirty years ago. The replacements are commercial products that provide the appearance of connection while delivering its opposite. This book documents the destruction of the institutions that made American social life functional, names the economic and policy forces that did the destroying, and traces the consequences for mental health, civic participation, and the basic human capacity to be known by other people.

The Theft of Childhood: How American Kids Stopped Becoming Adults

Children spend more time on screens than in any previous generation, less time outdoors than any previous generation, and reach standard milestones of independence later than any previous generation. The teen mental health collapse that accelerated after 2012 is not mysterious. The mechanism is documented. Phone-based childhood, helicopter parenting, the elimination of unsupervised play, the medicalization of normal developmental difficulty, and the school system's drift toward credentials over capacity have produced a generation that is anxious, fragile, and structurally unprepared for adulthood. This book names what was taken, who took it, and what would have to change for the next generation to get a different result.

Books by Richard Lowe

See books by Richard Lowe at
https://masterofworlds.com

Get free publishing insights and industry updates at
https://thewritingking.substack.com

For ghostwriting and book coaching services see
https://thewritingking.com

Index